Customer Service Intelligence

Customer Service Intelligence

Perspectives for Human Resources and Training

Lynn Van Der Wagen

Routledge
Taylor & Francis Group

LONDON AND NEW YORK

First published 2008 by Butterworth-Heinemann
Published 2016 by Routledge
2 Park Square, Milton Park, Abingdon, Oxon, OX14 4RN
711 Third Avenue, New York, NY 10017

Routledge is an imprint of the Taylor & Francis Group, an informa business

Notice
No responsibility is assumed by the publisher for any injury and/or damage to persons
or property as a matter of products liability, negligence or otherwise, or from any use
or operation of any methods, products, instructions or ideas contained in the material
herein.

British Library Cataloguing in Publication Data
A catalogue record for this book is available from the British Library

Library of Congress Cataloguing in Publication Data
A catalogue record for this book is available from the Library of Congress

ISBN: 978-0-7506-8190-2

Contents

Contents

Contents

Preface

Can the Zen concept of mindfulness inform customer service trainers? Can one select and train staff for their emotional intelligence? Does Skinner have anything useful to contribute with reinforcement theory? Vygotski talks about 'the object' which, in this case, is quality customer service, as being a dynamic and complex social action. This book brings together a wide range of historical and contemporary theories and uses them as the bases for different training approaches that can be applied by the professional trainer in numerous industry contexts.

During my career as a trainer, first in five star hotels and, more recently, working on the Olympic Games and other special event training projects, I have been vexed by the complete lack of formal attention given to training and development in service industries. By this I mean that everything appears to be quite ad hoc; a lot of time and money is allocated, with limited analysis and evaluation directed at increasing levels of service efficiency or professionalism. One of the issues that strikes me as most problematic is the variety of training contexts and the different demands that these place on a trainer. For example, Olympic Games training runs on a tight budget and the aim here is to develop service skills, including cultural and disability awareness, in a workforce of 110 000 people. This workforce comprises paid staff, volunteers, contractors and sponsor employees. Every one in this workforce needs to be au fait with all information relating to the Olympic Games and needs to be motivated to show off his or her home city to the best advantage. In these circumstances, where it is decided for example, that the organizers cannot afford to provide participants with a cup of tea and a biscuit (budget $50 000), training has to be streamlined and imaginative. The impact of this type of training is a feather touch. Despite this, it is supported by media hype and deeply held patriotism so that, when the opening ceremony begins, even normally surly train guards fall over their feet to provide the friendliest service. This turns the weeks of the Olympic Games into a magical period of bonhomie which evaporates as soon as the event is over. In comparison with this short training, at best a few hours, students in colleges are often allocated numerous subject hours and the trainer is faced with the problem of teaching customer service theory in an environment in which there are no customers! The customer service trainer, whether based in an organizational environment or a college, has to plan the scope of training, depth of training, level of simulation or realism, assessment of learning and evaluate the long-term training impacts. He or she needs to consider variations in customer service in a wide variety of industries, including for example, retail sales; health care; computing; hairdressing; policing and funeral services.

As a result of my experience across a number of such situations, I decided to turn to established theories of learning, emotional intelligence, leadership and motivation to see what we could learn. In this book, we look at customer service from a number of different theoretical perspectives in order to discuss the implications for training and development. Each chapter introduces a concept or model, uses it to enhance what we mean by customer service and then analyses what this might mean in the workplace for managers selecting and training their staff. These perspectives come from the social sciences, psychology and sociology with inclusion of management, leadership, motivation and communication theories. Of necessity, only pertinent elements are dealt with. For this reason, readers are encouraged to visit the works of the masters, Skinner, Bandura, Vygotski, Vroom and their colleagues further to extend their understanding of these important insights and their complexity.

I have been involved in vocational training for fifteen years and have searched for the holy grail, a perfect model for customer service delivery and a simple solution to developing staff who are skilled at customer service. This search has proved frustrating, particularly so in recent times where the competency movement has had such a strong influence over curriculum and training design in many countries, most notably the UK, Australia, New Zealand, Germany and Canada. In Australia, for example, I have recently reached the conclusion that the competency units developed for use in all industries have limited value to trainers. This will be explained further in Chapter Six where the merits of the system will be described too. Despite my current frustrations with this model, I have to confess to having been an advocate for this system for some time.

Autobiographical account of a training career

For readers who are embarking on a career in teaching or training, it may be interesting to look at the various assignments that I have undertaken during my career. These clearly demonstrate that a single approach will never succeed in such a wide range of training environments.

Affirmative action

The five star hotel in which I held my first job had a strong affirmative action program. This meant that we needed to develop a wide scope of training programs in literacy and 'coping with urban life' for the many rural workers arriving in the city for the first time. Learning curves were steep for some, but outcomes exceeded expectations with many of these participants reaching management positions over time. The political and organizational climate in which this occurred was fraught with debate and opposition to new initiatives. This was an organic learning organization in a climate of rapid political change.

Raising children (mine and others)

As any parent would know, teaching is a key parental role. One of the early lessons is that a child will not do things until ready: he won't walk until he is ready, won't talk until he is ready and won't read until he is ready. This is an important lesson in 'just in time' training. Vygotski (1962) calls this the zone promixal development or ZPD. Vygotski referred to the distance between the abilities displayed independently and those displayed with social support as the ZPD. This most widely known concept of his theory represents the distance between the actual level of development as determined by independent problem-solving [without guided instruction] and the level of potential development as determined by problem-solving under adult guidance or in collaboration with more capable peers. Because Vygotski asserts that cognitive change occurs within the zone of proximal development, instruction should be designed to reach a developmental level that is just above the learner's current level. If we consider that learning is a lifelong process then we are all in a zone of promixal development (although hopefully not the same one as last year!).

Workshops developing competency units

When the competency approach was emerging as a popular solution to national vocational training initiatives, I facilitated many workshops for industries, organizations and educational institutions who wanted to develop competency units for their professions. As I mentioned in the chapter on this topic, I soon learned that any debate on the topic 'what is competence?' was likely to derail the process, and generally forged ahead to develop standards that would be useful in practice. In particular, I was privileged to see one organization embed this process in their human resource development program and work closely with a university to collaborate on a parallel program. In contrast, I have experienced extreme frustration with some of the competency units as they have replaced curriculum in colleges. The focus on atomistic and oversimplified outcomes has been counterproductive in some areas.

Teaching apprentice chefs in a college

One of my first formal teaching experiences was with a group of apprentice chefs. I do hope they can't remember the lesson as it was right outside their ZPD. I shudder to remember how inappropriate the approach was, my inexperience in formal training was evident. This was an unforgettable lesson in finding out more about the participants and their learning needs.

Teaching hospitality management in a college

This led to some stimulating years as a teacher, the part I enjoyed the most was the opportunity it afforded to work with groups of students over long periods of six months or more and to see deep and meaningful learning in progress. Much of the assessment was workplace and project based.

Undertaking a training needs analysis

Working again for a hotel group I was asked to undertake a training needs analysis for the organization. Here the focus shifted to meeting business needs, in particular, short-term benefits to the organization such as efficiency, customer service and profitability. This was in a climate of high staff turnover, shift work and casualization. With such a transient workforce training was definitely a 'telling style' as described in Chapter Four. These employees all had low job maturity.

Training project for the Sydney 2000 Olympic Games

 This was going from bad to worse. Most hotel employees worked for up to three months as a minimum. In contrast, volunteers working at the Sydney Olympic Games would be employed for ten days at best. For most, the opportunity for training was limited to two short sessions (in groups of up to 3000) and one brief description of the specific tasks assigned to each individual. This was reductionism in the extreme and I have memories of trying to make fonts smaller and smaller just so that we could fit enough information in the volunteer pocket books. Training was short, sharp and focused with entertainment built in for motivation.

Writing management training materials for an international hotel group

Concurrently with the Games project, I was writing self-paced training manuals for managers at senior levels in yet another hotel organization. This was a significant contrast as the learning was linked to the context of the manager's work and a problem-solving approach was taken. The outcomes were fairly open-ended and the collaboration of a mentor was used as part of the experiential learning process. This long-term, career changing and context based program was extremely satisfying to develop.

Short-term consultancies and workshops

I have run a number of short-term consultancies and workshops in which there has always been a need to respond to the training brief provided by the client. The most memorable of these was one held on a Friday afternoon (after a big lunch) when I had already overheard employees grumbling about the fact that they knew everything there was to know about customer service. They were sure that any problems were the fault of management. In this climate, I was able to hook a few, but the rest went to sleep!

Formal presentations

Every trainer has to give formal presentations from time to time. Having watched many of these, I am always struck by the way in which a good speaker attains a high level of credibility even when the content is lacking. My problem is usually the opposite!

Teaching in China

Most recently I have taught Chinese students in Shanghai about tourism management. Here, the social and educational environment is different. Scaffolding, as described in Chapter Seven, has been extremely helpful in my efforts to move away from didactic methods and work with these students on applied tasks.

Sharan Merriam explains this well and reinforces my thinking:

> While a grand theory of adult learning might seem to make our task easier in explaining our field to others, it would have to be so broad it would ultimately explain nothing. A much more vibrant model is what we have now – a prism of theories, ideas and frameworks that allows us to see the same phenomenon from different angles. (Merriam 1998, p. 96)

As this author points out, there are three ways in which all of these approaches are contributing to our understanding of adult learning. First, the learner is seen as a whole being, and learning incorporates experience, emotion, cognition and imagination. Second, learning is seen as a process, it is transformative. Sometimes how we learn is more important that what we learn. Finally, context is vitally important. Learning is part of being socially, culturally and historically situated.

Thus, having spent a career in vocational training, and having been enthused at one time or another by various books and theories, I am finally reaching a stage of age and wisdom (the former without doubt, the latter one can only hope), where I am realizing that each of these models provides a different and valuable perspective. As with the leadership theorists in the 1970s, I am reaching the conclusion that there is no 'best way'. A trainer needs a training toolkit to work as a practitioner in the development of professional customer service. Depending on the training context, factors such as the type of business, level of interaction with customer, diversity of employee and customer base and variety of products, different perspectives and tools can contribute in different ways to training effectiveness.

My hope is that on reading this book, you will find that at each chapter you exclaim, 'this is it!' only to move onto the next chapter and realize that this too has a contribution to make to your understanding of your role as a trainer. This book is titled 'Customer Service Intelligence' as it acknowledges that there is nothing simple about service. As a form of human communication, service is extremely complex, it is unique to social and historical situations as well as to specific contexts in which the service provider and customer interact.

References

Merriam, S.B. (1998) *Qualitative research and case study applications in education.* Jossey-Bass, San Francisco.

Vygotski, L.S. (1962) *Thought and language.* MIT Press, Cambridge.

Acknowledgements

The author would like to acknowledge the contributions of the following people and organisations:

Australian National Training Authority (now National Training Information Service); Australasian Centre for Policing Research; Daily Telegraph; Hilton Group; Singapore Press; TAFE NSW; University Southern Queensland.

Valentina McInerney (a delightful and encouraging reader); Ian Cornford; Yrjö Engeström; Dominque Rychen; Lesley Guthrie; and the team that produced the book Eleanor Blow; Annie Powell; Angela Brennan; Olivia Warburten; Ailsa Marks; and Melissa Read.

The organizations listed above gave permission for me to use their material. Every effort has been made to trace the owners of copyright material, in some cases with limited success, and I offer apologies to any copyright holders whose rights I may have unwittingly infringed.

Introduction

Chapter One will cover the all important overview of instructional design. For training to be effective, it needs to have a clear direction, it needs to be planned and purposeful. This chapter looks at the idea of training games and ice-breakers and the way they are used in training. This chapter goes further to look at two approaches to training, direct instruction and facilitated training. The first of these is most suited to situations in which information is transmitted to the audience, such as new product information and marketing campaigns. The second of these is a much more open-ended approach in which the trainer helps individuals and groups to construct new knowledge and concepts. This is followed by Chapter Two which looks at the idea of 'product' in more detail and suggests that if the service product needs to be differentiated then unique approaches to training are required.

Chapter Three will discuss the attributes that the employee brings to the service interaction and will introduce the concept of emotional intelligence (Goleman, 1995). The use of selection instruments (pre-employment screening questionnaires) will be discussed in terms of their validity and reliability. Moving on from the affective domain and discussion about personality attributes, Chapter Four will deal with the behaviourist theories of Skinner (1953) in which the consequences of behaviour are used to reinforce learning. These principles are widely used for skill development and can be extended to cover behaviour modification and modelling (Bandura, 1969, 1977). Two-dimensional models, the basis for many leadership theories, will be reviewed in Chapter Five. The study of motivation and leadership has a lot to offer anyone responsible for managing customer service systems. In particular, the framework offered by Victor Vroom (1973) enables us to look at the perceptions of the learners, their expectations of success or failure, and the value they place on the benefits of learning. This theory is known as expectancy theory. As trainers, we often make the assumption, incorrect in some cases, that the learning goals are achievable and the outcomes valuable. Looking instead at the learners' perceptions as they influence their goal setting can be insightful.

The competency movement with its focus on outcomes will be the topic of Chapter Six, along with a brief review of contemporary thinking and implications for approaches to training and recognition of prior learning. Chapter Seven will take us into a discussion about research and theorizing in the area of expertise and its development, mainly with a focus on cognitive development. This brings us to Chapter Eight in which sociocultural theories are used to emphasize the importance of context 'situatedness' and this is elaborated further. As in all chapters, the implications for customer service training will be discussed, in this case with the perspective that service delivery is a team effort and training should involve a collaborative social group. A much more complex model of human behaviour developed by Vygotsky and contemporary Russian theorists including Leont'ev (1981 (1959)) will emerge in Chapter Nine as one of the most valuable approaches for analysis. Customer service will be described in this chapter as an 'object', something dynamic and not static, influenced by a range of factors illustrated in the model presented. Of significance here is the concept of artefacts or tools which are used in, and influence, communication. In the customer service context the artefacts can include, for example, a menu, computer software, a company slogan etc. Further, the theory stresses that all forms of communication are culturally and historically situated.

In Chapter Ten, the final perspective that will be introduced is that of mindfulness, a Buddhist concept, more recently adapted for communication theory and business management.

References

Bandura, A. (1969) *Principles of behaviour modification*. Holt, Rinehart and Winston, New York.

Bandura, A. (1977) *Social learning theory*. Prentice Hall, Englewood Cliffs.

Goleman, D. (1995) *The emotionally intelligent workplace*. Bantam Books, New York.

Leont'ev, A. (1981) (1959) *Problems of the development of the mind*. Progress Publishers, Moscow.

Skinner, B.F. (1953) *Science and human behaviour*. Macmillan, New York.

Vroom, V. (1973) *Work and motivation*. John Wiley and Sons, New York.

Vygotski, L.S. (1962) *Thought and language*. MIT Press, Cambridge.

Training Design

There are some disadvantages to the use of games. The game can be too simplistic and therefore provide an incomplete or inaccurate view of reality. Since the game is played for fun, trainees may not take them seriously. Decisions and actions will be treated lightly since they have no consequences in real life. Because some of the objectives are often hidden, participants may leave a training session unaware of what was learned. For these reasons, the game must be carefully designed to meet training objectives. The trainer must play a key role in setting the stage at the beginning of the game and leading a post-game discussion to be sure the objectives were met.

Read and Kleiner, 1996, p. 735

Central theme

Activity based training is currently in vogue. In some cases, the activity is an ice-breaker, while in others it is an outdoor team building exercise. The activity selected for high level participation must be planned with the aims of the programme in mind. It is not appropriate for participants to leave customer service training having had fun but having learned nothing that will transfer to the workplace.

Training recommendations

1 The organizational aims of any customer service training program must be considered. These are generally linked to strategic and operational planning.

2 The profiles and needs of learners are a further consideration. The group may be a ready made team or a diverse group of people who do not know each other and come from a variety of different backgrounds.

3 Depending on the aims of the program, the trainer needs to think about the training methods. There are a number of possibilities which need to be carefully selected.

4 Sessions can involve direct transmission of information, such as product information. In other cases or phases of training, the trainer takes on a completely different role, that of facilitator assisting with the development of new concepts and courses of action that cannot be specified in advance of the programme.

5 Flexibility and a capacity to modify training techniques in response to the situation and participants are vitally important. Many programs blend a range of training techniques.

6 Training involves a starting point, a journey and an end point. This needs to be articulated and managed by the trainer. A sense of progress in learning is the positive outcome that is the ideal.

This chapter will highlight some of the variables that a trainer might consider during the design phase of programme development. In light of the theme of this book, which is that there is no 'one size fits all' approach to customer service training, it is appropriate that consideration is given to the following questions:

■ What is the area of instruction?

■ What are the training needs or goals for learning?

■ Are there specific learning objectives?

■ Who is the audience and what are their characteristics?

■ Do the learners have a preferred learning style?

■ How homogeneous or differentiated is the audience?

■ What physical space is available?

■ Which methods of instruction are most appropriate?

■ What tasks need to be performed?

■ What assessment methods will be used?

■ What opportunities are there for practice during and after training?

■ How will training effectiveness be evaluated?

This last question is often framed in the form of a 'happy sheet' which is answered at the end of the training session. Many trainees leave customer service training saying, 'I had fun' and this is seen as an indicator of a successful program. Seemingly, the greatest fear of any workplace trainer is that participants say that they were bored. For this and many other reasons, a current trend is for training to involve games and participation exercises. The efficacy of these and other training approaches need to be considered carefully in the training design phase.

The worst feedback a trainer can get is 'I didn't learn anything' or 'what was that about?'

Learners must have fun?

Most workplace trainers have an immediate priority which is to stimulate and energize participants. As a result, activity based training games have become extremely popular. Gary Kroehnert's popular '100 Training Games' (1991) has been followed by a sequel '103 Additional Training Games' (2001) and there are many more on the market including 'The Big Book of Customer Service Training Games' by Carlaw and Deming (1999). However, many games do not meet instructional goals. For this reason, it is important to consider design issues and to use these to establish a map for everyone concerned, trainers and participants. One characteristic of adult learners is that they like to know what is expected and how the training will evolve. Adult learners are also able to see the difference between fun for fun's sake and active learning in which they are emotionally involved and intellectually challenged by new ideas. They are also able to develop new concepts and try out new approaches or behaviours. The active part of the training program is thus much more than entertainment. This is not to say that ice-breakers do not have a part to play in developing motivation and camaraderie. However, experiential learning involves

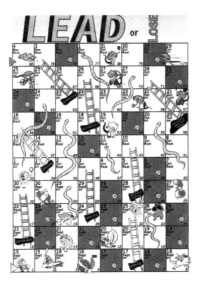

immersing learners in environments in which they acquire knowledge through situational interaction (Feinstein et al., 2002) and for this to be successful it needs to be purposeful.

Approaches to learning

While this book does not attempt to discuss theoretical approaches to learning in any detail, it is helpful for the customer service trainer to consider two approaches that tend to polarize thinking in this field.

First, direct instruction is used to transmit information to the learner, as for example in the case of a university lecture given to a large audience. A considerable part of classroom instruction in primary and secondary schools is also characterized by this direct approach. Rote learning forms the basis for learning in many environments and cultures. In China, for example, a student learns to write many different characters through practice and repetition. Full literacy involves learning between three and four thousand characters in a writing system that appeared over 3000 years ago. In the workplace, direct instruction is used in a variety of ways: during orientation training to provide new employees with information about the organization and its structure; during on-job training to explain and demonstrate new products and procedures; and during meetings when updated information is provided. The analogy that is often used for this is that of the learner as an empty vessel into which information is poured. Kivinen and Ristela refer to this as 'telling and listening' (2003, p. 372).

If one considers the agenda for an orientation session for new organizational recruits it might follow the following outline:

- Introduction to the company and its mission

- History of the company

- Customers and products

- Customer service

- Occupational health and safety issues

- Grievance and other procedures

- Employee schemes and benefits.

During this time, the new employees are generally passive recipients of the information and their retention of this information is seldom tested. However, high performing employees are those who demonstrate a capacity to learn this information quickly, such as product features and benefits, and pass this information on to consumers.

The second philosophical approach taken to learning is that of constructivism. This perspective stresses the goals and activities of the learner and suggests that knowledge is personally constructed and cannot be delivered in exact form from one person to another. From a constructivist perspective, the goal for learning is the creation of context-dependent, flexible and adaptive learning and problem-solving. The analogy of building is also used, as it is in this text in the later chapter on scaffolding. To design training with this in mind, the trainer would:

- Use authentic and complex tasks as the basis for instruction

- Support the learner in developing ownership and self-regulation

- Facilitate learning by challenging thinking and ideas

- Provide opportunities for testing alternatives

- Encourage reflection on action.

Finally, this perspective stresses the social environment in which people learn, an environment which is often highly unpredictable.

In practice

The Hilton Group, with 500 hotels, devised a new service concept to set its service apart – *Equilibrium*. The purpose of Equilibrium is to ensure that all Hilton customers enjoy a restorative stay that helps to balance work and leisure needs. Their training program, *Esprit* (which delivers this quality service initiative), is described as follows:

'A philosophy, an ethos that nurtures the intuitive service that is Equilibrium' (*Hilton hits the heights of hotel service with HR initiative*, 2004, p. 24).

Questions

1 In a group, discuss your personal perspectives on work and leisure balance.

2 How could a hotel meet your needs for work/leisure balance?

3 As a trainer how would you feel about designing training for a marketing program that is so heavily reliant on customers' perceptions?

4 Contrast six professions in which customer service is highly intuitive, and six in which it is not.

Training methods

When developing a training program, the trainer needs to decide on content, sequence, and training methods. Burns (1996) refers to the trainer's 'range of acts', suggesting that training is a performance and that presenters need a range of acts which can contribute to their repertoire, including acting, dancing, singing, weight training and playing instruments. Volunteer training, counselling and participating in weekend army reserve are also activities that can increase awareness of the diversity of training contexts and participant groups. These are some examples of ways in which trainers can develop specific skills and analyse instructional approaches in a range of instructional environments.

Methods of instruction can include, for example:

- Lecture

- Demonstration

- Case study

- Simulation

- Game

- Problem-solving exercise

- Group discussion

- Structured exercise

- Field trip

- Role play

- Collaborative learning

- Coaching and scaffolding.

Feinstein et al. (2002) differentiate between role play and game play:

> Role play allows participants to immerse themselves in a learning environment by acting out the role of a character and part in a particular situation. The participant follows a set of rules that defines the situation and then interacts with others who are also role playing. This learning activity allows participants to get an in-depth understanding of many of the social interactions that arise when evaluating or solving a problem (p. 735).

According to these authors, gaming consists of interactions between players who are constrained by rules and procedures but exclude acting. The focus for game playing is usually decision-making, not social interaction.

Planned and purposeful

The argument presented in this chapter is that training should be planned and purposeful. Even when the training is relatively open-ended and the trainer's role is to facilitate the development of new ideas or procedures, a framework is still needed. The learners need to move from attention to action.

Establish interest

Participants in training need to be motivated. They need to see that the learning will be interesting, relevant and applicable.

Identify the goals

People want to know where they are going and understand the journey they are undertaking. This requires a map and an outline against which progress can be measured.

Explain and monitor process and progress

The trainer needs to monitor the learning process, carefully facilitating so that too many tangents are not explored. Those that are useful and meaningful should be elaborated.

Give examples of concepts

As a facilitator of learning, one of the most useful things that the instructor does is assist with the articulation of ideas and concepts. This requires a deep knowledge of the topic and context.

Provide demonstration or examples

Examples bring meaning to concepts. Case studies and problems can be used to illustrate concepts. These can be in the form of customer complaints, mystery customer reports, competitor information, market research, personal experience and anecdotes. Jokes, games and role play can play a meaningful part in training if linked to these emerging concepts.

Link new concepts with ones that are familiar

Learners need to attach new ideas to something they understand. They need to see how these concepts apply to their circumstances.

Expand thinking

For a learner, challenge is something that needs to occur at just the right time. There is a tension between linking ideas to things that are familiar and leaping into territory that is new for the learner so, for the learner, timing is crucial.

Consolidate new concepts or procedures

The learner needs the opportunity for practice. This may be in the physical sense of learning a skill or it may be a cognitive process, where the learner is engaged actively and reflectively. In the customer service field applied tasks can include:

- Developing aims for customer service

- Developing a positioning statement (against competitors)

- Responding to customer objections (a well-known strategy in selling)

- Developing new product (goods and services) ideas

- Planning service procedures.

As Kivinen and Ristela (2003) point out:

> although there are phases in studying that require little overt activity, the whole cycle of learning involves also experimentation, trying one's ideas out

on things and discovering what can be done with materials and appliances, not to forget means-consequences reflection (p. 373).

In the chapters that follow, readers will first look at customer service from a marketing perspective and will be provided with a smorgasbord of ideas for customer service training in different organizational contexts.

Summary

Learners are motivated by customer service programmes that are activity based, are flexible and offer variety. From a design perspective, the trainer must ensure that the methods of instruction selected from a vast array of possibilities are the most suitable. Of course, the approach is not guaranteed and nothing is certain. The instructional methods selected are those *most likely* to work. Selecting the right mix of training approaches is very challenging and effective trainers need to remain flexible as there are many occasions on which the direction of the programme changes in response to learner needs. The programme must meet the needs of the individual learner and the organization in both the short and longer term. Direct instruction is less complex to manage than facilitated training that is less clear about the specific outcomes of training.

Case Study

The following case study discusses the importance of customer service provided by library staff and the training initiatives that were undertaken to improve the level of training.

The quest to improve client service at the University of Southern Queensland (USQ) Library began in the mid to late 1990s. At that time, comments and results from Client Congruence surveys revealed that the service offered by the Library was not always meeting client expectations. There were some negative comments about services and about service staff being rude and unhelpful. The Loans Desk introduced a slogan of 'Service with a Smile' to encourage staff to be more approachable, friendly and helpful. This scheme met with instant success. By the 2000 survey, negative comments about staff had reduced significantly.

However, the new millennium has placed new demands on Library staff. The Library environment is now one which undergoes constant technological change and is faced with an ever increasing amount of information available in a variety of formats.

Academic libraries now play host to information commons and demanding generation Y students. It was soon realized that 'service with a smile' might get clients to the desk, but that staff needed to be better prepared to function effectively in the new environment.

While many staff realize the benefit of attending training, the mixture of comments received on the survey indicates that some staff see training as an addendum to, and distraction from, their work. The Library Training Working Party needs to promote the necessity of training more heavily to management and staff, to propagate a culture which views training as much a component of work as attending a meeting or doing a rostered desk shift. The working party hopes that the change in training times to regular fortnightly training sessions will encourage training to be viewed as a normal work occurrence. Some negative staff attitude towards training was due to staff compulsorily having to attend some training which they regarded as unnecessary. In most cases there was an identified reason (such as unacceptable error rates in records in the Library Management System) that prompted trainers to make sessions compulsory. In the future, varied approaches to training will be taken which take into account differing ability levels and learning styles. The Library Training Working Party will be encouraging trainers not immediately to choose a 1 hour lecture style or classroom style presentation, but to look at all the possibilities for training that are available, such as self-paced tutorials, one on one or small group training. For compulsory sessions that staff may not be keen to attend, trainers will be encouraged to consider the previous experience of trainees and ensure that all participants feel they are gaining knowledge, perhaps by streaming sessions into refresher sessions and more in-depth sessions.

Gaining managerial support is key to the success of the training programme. Initial concerns from some managers over the activities of the Working Party have been overcome by ensuring constant communication. Reports are presented monthly to the Library Management Committee which outline details of recent training, planned training and progress on other activities.

(Callow and Mullholland, 2005)

Questions

1 Employees are often cynical and resistant to training with customer service as the main topic. Discuss your experiences with this issue.

2 How was the training in this situation matched to the needs of participants?

3 Discuss the approach you would take to briefing the Library Management Committee about prospective customer training initiatives.

4 Discuss your general approach to instructional design in this case and compare it with the approach you might take to training novice employees in another industry or sector.

References

Burns, S. (1996) *Artistry in training: thinking differently about the way you help people to learn.* Woodslane, Warriewood.

Callow, M. and Mullholland, D. (2005) Service with a smile only gets you so far. Staff training for success in the integrated service environment. *neXt 2005: ALIA National Library & Information Technicians Conference*, Brisbane.

Carlaw, P. and Deming, V.K. (1999) *The big book of customer service training games: quick, fun activities for training customer service reps, salespeople, and anyone else who deals with customers.* McGraw-Hill, New York.

Feinstein, A., Mann, S. and Corsun, D. (2002) Charting the experiential territory: clarifying definitions and uses of computer simulation, games and role play. *Journal of Management Development*, 21(10), 732–744.

Hilton hits the heights of hotel service with HR initiative (2004) *Human Resource Management*, 24–26.

Kivinen, O. and Ristela, P. (2003) From constructivism to a pragmatist conception of learning. *Oxford Review of Education*, **29**(3), 371–374.

Kroehnert, G. (1991) *100 training games*. McGraw-Hill Australia, Sydney.

Kroehnert, G. (2001) *103 Additional Training Games*. McGraw-Hill Australia, Sydney.

Read, C. and Kleiner, B. (1996) Which training methods are effective? *Management Development Review*, **9**(2), 24–29.

2

Services Marketing

Nordstrom's success is down to a concentration on delivering outstanding customer service and the recognition that the best way to do this is not through a rule-book, but through empowering customer oriented employees. This is about more freedom and less about control; about recognizing the potential of people and not trying to define behaviour through systems. In terms of customer service it's almost impossible to use Taylorist scientific management principles to specify how employees should behave in all situations. Nor is it desirable. Customers want an individualized experience that matches their specific needs and wants. At a hygiene factor level that may be about systems, but at a differentiated level it is mostly about the quality of service. For that to occur employees need to identify with and be committed to the organization and its ideology.

Inside out: how employees build value, Nicholas Ind, Equilibrium Consulting
http://www.brandrevival.net/articles.html

Central theme

Customer service is a significant part of what marketing experts call 'the product', which is designed to meet customers' needs and wants. Customer service research has been dominated by marketing theorists whose main interest is the perception of service quality by the consumer and the consumer's subsequent purchase decisions and actions. In this book, the spotlight falls on the service provider. The marketing concepts of variability and inseparability associated with service delivery highlight first the uniqueness of each interaction between customer and service provider, and second the inseparability of the service from the service provider. Both concepts point to the importance of training and leadership for appropriate, consistent and efficient service delivery.

Training implications

1 The service interaction is a social act, unique in almost every instance, with participation by both service provider and customer.

2 Perceptions are developed by customers about their expectations and the service delivered – including gaps between these two perceptions.

3 Perceptions are developed by service providers (staff) about what customers expect and how satisfied they may be with the service provided.

4 There may or may not be consistency between the perceptions of the customer and that of the service provider about the quality or outcome of the service.

5 Customers have expectations about human dimensions of service, including the willingness to help and empathy of the service provider.

6 The service provider needs to understand and use systems and procedures in order to carry out seamless and sometimes invisible processes.

7 Organizations need to provide adequate personnel, equipment, facilities and systems to support service provision.

8 Quality service cannot be managed in the same way as quality control on a production line, rather human resource management processes, including training, are vitally important in an environment where the service is intangible, variable and inseparable.

Introduction

There is extensive writing on the topic of customer service, although it must be said that much of it is at the level of 'four easy steps to customer satisfaction' (Levesque, 2006). This oversimplification is not helpful. Providing an outstanding level of customer service involves complex communication, adaptive behaviour and expert judgment (McColl-Kennedy and White, 1997; Bove and Johnson, 2000; Sturdy, 2000). Furthermore, most of the research has been undertaken in the fields of marketing and consumer behaviour where the customer perspective has been dominant. This chapter will look at customer service from a marketing perspective and then from an organizational development and, more specifically, a training perspective. Having set the scene, the aim of the chapters that follow is to provide frameworks and techniques for customer service trainers by creating a trainer's toolkit that can be used in a variety of training contexts.

The contemporary environment

Before looking in more detail at the convergence of contemporary ideas in marketing and human resource management, a quick overview of the current service environment is in order. In most western countries, over half the workforce is employed in service industries and there has been a significant decline in primary industries (such as agriculture) and secondary industries (such as manufacturing). In the UK, for example, one in five jobs is in financial and business services (Argyris, 1993). Consumer expectations have changed following increases in disposable income, smaller families, changing lifestyles, greater consumer choice, greater mobility and aging populations. One of the most significant changes has been brought about by the level of information provided to customers on the Internet and the opportunity provided for online purchase. This medium is frequently used for product research, decision-making, buying goods unseen, writing complaints, seeking help etc. The following examples demonstrate some of the issues that service providers deal with every day:

My father passed away in January and we have spent six months trying to get the phone company to remove his name from the bill. This month it was finally amended. The next day a letter arrived from the phone company addressed to Dad: 'Dear Peter, we notice you have recently left us. We would like to have you back'. So would we!

I am writing to congratulate you for your efficiency. I have been banking with you for eight years and have never had such speedy service. It took you 30 minutes from the time my builder presented my check to the time you dishonored it and charged me a $50 penalty. My salary was deposited in the account, as it has been for the past eight years (96 times without fail) one hour after this check was presented.

Can I just thank you? If your company's policy is over-the-top incredible customer service and accountability, you have fulfilled it in spades, and I really appreciate it. Your response made my day, and made me feel so much more secure about ordering over the Internet (at least at your site). And it is really nice to know a name, and feel that you are working with a real person, just as you would in a store.

'I am not happy with my Internet service.'
'What is the problem Mrs Eddy?'
'When I click on the windows explorer e, the frame opens too small and I can't see the entire Internet.'

To overbook a short-haul flight by 30 seats is not a simple mistake: over-booking is a deliberate airline policy designed to prevent wasted capacity on flight but to this degree it demonstrates gross incompetence and a shocking lack of consideration for passenger needs. I am familiar with the operation of automated booking systems and know that it is difficult to overbook even a single seat without the system issuing warnings to the operator. The extent of this overbooking would have been known to the airline for hours or even days ahead of check-in. Alternative arrangements could have been prepared in anticipation of all of the passengers turning up for the flight. Had this been a budget airline, pathetic service, incompetence, rude staff and an abject failure to take responsibility might have been understandable. . . .

"I was in earlier and got overcharged 37 cents. I won't stand for it. You, sir, have no idea who you're dealing with."

The Internet is also widely used to make public complaints with many forums of the complain.com variety. There is no doubt that e-commerce has created dramatic changes in consumer behaviour requiring organizations to respond proactively.

Perception

As mentioned previously, most services marketing research involves analysis of customer perception. Perception is a personal filter used to interpret the things we experience.

> Perception is the process by which we take in, organize and give meaning to internal and external stimuli (Robbins, 2004).

Perception is thus selective. Short cuts, such as stereotyping (in marketing this is known as customer segmentation), while often time saving, can also be counterproductive. There are many well-known perceptual processes such as the halo effect, projection, attribution and expectancy. Images such as the vase/faces and inkblot shown in the practical exercise that follows can stimulate discussion about individual perceptions leading on to discussions about attitudes and values.

Figure 2.1 Perception. Inkblot test

In practice

Review the above two images in a small group.

Questions

1 Discuss the various interpretations of the illustrations made by members of your group.

2 What are the implications of this for customer service?

3 As a group, share your experiences and perceptions of service you have experienced.

Classifying services

There have been many attempts to classify services but, as Nankervis (2005a, p. 16) suggests, 'the immense size, fragmentation and amorphous nature of services, and the dynamic relationship between services providers, defy simplistic definitions of their boundaries or components'. Lovelock and Wirtz (2004) illustrate this with the following four dimensions:

- services that act on people's minds (such as education, psychology)

- services that act on people's bodies (such as transportations, medicine, massage)

- services that act on people's belongings (such as cleaning, repairs)

- services that act on people's information (such as taxation, banking, insurance).

There are, however, many different service classification models. These look primarily at the nature of the service provided, such as the classification just described, at the extent of customer contact and the service process. Sometimes service is routine and other times extremely complex. For example, in some cases the service routine is scripted as in, 'Can I have a large fries please?' and the unthinking response, 'Would you like fries with that?' In others, there is an extraordinary level of complexity in the service provided, such as a psychologist counselling a person who has been experiencing psychotic episodes or a police officer helping at the scene of an accident. As these examples illustrate, one could also classify services in terms of the commercial and non-commercial organizations providing the service.

In practice

Develop a method of classifying the following services:

- Plumbing
- Massage
- Physiotherapy
- Car sales
- Hairdressing
- Wedding planning
- Financial planning
- Premises cleaning
- Furniture sales
- Internet provider
- Real estate
- Tourism

Services marketing

Marketing is a process of production and exchange that is concerned with the flow of goods and services from producer to consumer. Goods or commodities differ from services in that they are manufactured, tangible and more easily subject to quality control. On the other hand, services, such as those provided by a travel agency, are less tangible. For this reason, services marketing provides more challenges, particularly since the service provided is the key part of the product. Goods and services are marketed as products in various combinations along a continuum. Some products are clearly commodities (goods), such as a loaf of bread. At the other end of the spectrum, massage therapy is clearly a service. However, in the middle of the spectrum, there are products that combine goods and services such as restaurant meals. Here the food is the commodity and the waiting staff provide the service. Depending on the type of restaurant, ranging from fast food to fine dining, the restaurant would sit at different places on the goods/services continuum. This is illustrated in Figure 2.2.

A review of services marketing would be deficient if the leading instrument developed by Parasuraman et al. (Zeithaml et al., 1990; Zeithaml et al., 1991; Parasuraman et al., 1998) was not discussed. These authors have had a long and ongoing impact with their research. Indeed, these authors have developed the most widely used definition of service quality as 'meeting customer expectations' (Parasuraman et al., 1998, p. 12) and they clearly differentiate between goods and services, services having the characteristics of intangibility, heterogeneity and inseparability. These three characteristics are described here as they are widely used in services marketing theory and have implications for customer service training.

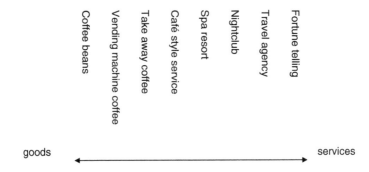

Figure 2.2 The goods and services continuum

Intangibility refers to the fact that services cannot be touched and are hard to anticipate. This is in contrast to goods which occupy space and have various tangible qualities, 'services consist of social acts or interactions and exist in time only' (Berry and Clark, 1980). Indeed, 'most services actually consist of acts and interactions, which are typically social events' (Sureschchandar et al., 2001). Inseparability refers to the concurrent creation and consumption of the product. Service is created in a social encounter, not on a production line. It is thus difficult to control quality in the same way that one might do for goods in production. The service provided is also inseparable from the service provider and, indeed, some might argue, also inseparable from the customer who plays a participating role in the shifting and changing perceptions on both sides of the service interaction. Finally, services are variable, in that most are unique communications, with customer perceptions differing from day to day and from minute to minute. These characteristics all point to the importance of training as one part of the human resources strategy to provide a skilled, knowledgeable and proactive workforce.

The original and revised SERVQUAL (Zeithaml et al., 1990) surveys contain five dimensions: tangibles; reliability; responsiveness; assurance; and empathy. The tangibles refer to the physical dimensions of the company and the product environment, for example, décor and equipment. The remaining four dimensions focus largely on the human aspects of service delivery. Sureschchandar et al. (2001) debate the comprehensiveness of the survey and the balance between human aspects of service delivery and the tangibles of service with the human aspects dominating the 'servicescape'.

Some examples from the survey relating to the human aspects of delivery include:

- dependability in handling customer service problems

- keeping customers informed

- willingness to help customers

- readiness to respond to customer requests

- employees who instill confidence in customers

- employees who are consistently courteous

- employees who have the knowledge to answer customer questions

- giving customers individual attention

- employees who deal with customers in a caring fashion

- having the customers' best interests at heart

- providing services at the promised time.

The efficacy of SERVQUAL has been questioned for many reasons, including the reliability and validity of the instrument when used across different settings (organizations and cultures). However, in the most relevant of these papers, Sureschchandar et al. point to the absence of focus on systematization of service delivery. The point they make is that no matter how convivial the service provider, this does not lead to customer satisfaction if the core service is not seamless from a systems point of view. They refer to this as the 'CONTENT' of service (p. 115). For example, no matter how well treated, travellers will not be happy with airline service if the plane is late or judged unsafe. Likewise, banking staff cannot meet the needs of customers through the force of their smiling personalities if the system cannot deliver an insurance policy within a given time and specification. Their point is well made and brings to mind the seminal work of Herzberg (1959) in motivation theory where he identifies 'satisfiers' and 'hygiene factors' (things one would normally expect and take for granted unless lacking), the first leading to satisfaction and the second to dissatisfaction.

Sureschchandar et al. (2001) identify the following dimensions for systemization of the core service or content of delivery:

- having highly standardized and simplified delivery process so that services are delivered without any hassles or excessive bureaucracy

- having a highly simplified and structured delivery process so that the service delivery times are minimum

- enhancement of technological capability to serve customers more efficiently

- degree to which the procedures and processes are perfectly foolproof

- adequate and necessary personnel for good customer service

- adequate and necessary facilities for good customer service
(Sureschchandar et al., 2001, p. 118).

In the hospitality industry in the USA, SERVQUAL is widely used, with modifications, to meet the needs of the lodging (accommodation) sector and the restaurant sector (Stevenson, 2003). These instruments have been validated by confirmatory factor analysis.

Two studies that looked at the problem of the use of instruments such as SERVQUAL have been conducted in China, looking at Chinese cultural values in the dining experience, and in the UK, where the perceptions of Japanese tourists staying in hotels were analysed. Both studies found that service expectations are culture specific. In China, *mien-tsu* is a form of social currency, a sense of prestige and honor obtained from others, in this case in the service encounter (Tsai, 2004). This expectation is weighted highly in China and this part of service valued highly. In the second study, Japanese tourists staying in the UK rated Japanese culture-specific services as a requirement and a gap emerged in the expectation–delivery survey. It was found that international guests have different or greater service expectations than do their British counterparts (Osawa and Ball, 2003).

Differentiated service

Marketing research contributes to our understanding of customer service in that it highlights the importance of customers' expectations and perceptions, as well as emphasizing the social nature of any interaction with service personnel. Work done on SERVQUAL, and many subsequent reviews, continue to modify and improve this instrument for international application. However, the issue of cultural differences remains. The debate over whether customers expect an internationally homogenized style of service or look forward to a unique service experience will continue to confound those who develop service products and this, in turn, will have implications for workplace trainers who prepare people to deliver a particular style of service. 'Product differentiation' is a much espoused mantra of marketing gurus and in service industries this means service differentiation. Following this line of thinking, training for differentiated service cannot follow simple or popular formulas. In marketing terms product differentiation is defined as follows:

> A policy which emphasizes those *features* which distinguish one *product* from other similar *products*. The practice of making one *product* distinguishable from all other products in the minds of consumers.

Thus, to deliver a service that is unique, the trainer must develop:

A training programme which emphasizes those features which distinguish one service from other similar services.

Organizational training and development

Customer service training, while the ultimate responsibility of the immediate supervisor in most establishments, is part of the organization's human resources and organizational development strategy. Training is a human resources function in organizations. In large organizations, the training plan is developed and managed by a human resources or training and development specialist. However, the responsibility for training rests with the direct line of supervision and management. Front line managers are responsible for on-job performance and, ultimately, the bottom line impact of satisfactory or unsatisfactory performance. For organizations, this split responsibility for training (staff and line) is problematic as there is often limited transfer from off job training to on job performance. The challenge for training specialists is to plan training that is integrated with ongoing business operations, relevant and timely. For most organizations, training also has to show a bottom line benefit or return on investment (Nankervis et al., 2002; Nankervis, 2005b). In the case of small business, training is seldom isolated as a discrete role, but is a functional responsibility of all senior staff. Skill transfer is less problematic as most training occurs on the job, in context and under close supervision.

Training is generally linked to organizational vision, strategy and product development. While many organizations see training as a solution to service deficiencies, there may be numerous operational hurdles that stand in the way of quality service such as poor equipment, workflow planning, supervision or discipline. Training is not a discrete, stand alone option, it is part of strategic planning and needs to be fully integrated into policies, procedures, standards and evaluation plans to work successfully.

Human resources strategies that support service delivery include:

- Job design
- Recruitment
- Selection

- Induction

- Training

- Performance management

- Motivation and compensation.

With respect to the current trend towards competency based training, Nankervis et al. (2005) suggest that 'organizations must develop their own competencies rather than adopt those of another organization or, has happens in many cases, buy off-the-shelf competency packages from consultancies' (Nankervis et al., 2005, p. 278). The authors compare the competency approach to the fashionable trait approach of the first half of the twentieth century which was discredited by contingency theorists. Contingency theory will be discussed further in the forthcoming discussions regarding contemporary management and leadership approaches in the services sector.

Summary

This chapter has described, somewhat briefly, marketing and consumer behaviour approaches to quality service. The Human Resource Management function of training has also been introduced since the convergence of services marketing research and organizational behaviour research is the focus of this book. In particular, this chapter has highlighted the unique features of services marketing: intangibility, variability and inseparability. The conclusion we reach at this early stage is that there is nothing simple about customer service!

> ### On reflection
>
> The following two newspaper extracts cover Singapore's customer service training targeted at 21 000 tourism personnel and one hotel employee's response to the initiative which he says is a waste of money.
>
> **S'poreans get an 'F' for courtesy**
> T. Rajan
> 21 June 2006

Singapore was placed a dismal 30 out of 35 cities in a Reader's Digest courtesy test, showing it still has a long way to go – even after more than a quarter century of courtesy campaigns.

New York finished tops in the three tests: holding a door open, saying 'thank you', and helping someone pick up dropped items. Joining it at the top were Zurich in Switzerland and Canada's Toronto in second and third place.

Languishing at the bottom of the list with Singapore were South Korean capital Seoul, Kuala Lumpur, India's financial centre, Mumbai, Bucharest in Romania and Moscow.

The only thing Singaporeans have to smile about was the good score for service standards. Seventy per cent of staff at retailers surveyed – from classy Marks & Spencer to mamak, or corner shops – said 'please' and 'thank you' before and after a purchase.

The Singapore segment of the survey, the first global poll done by Reader's Digest, was conducted over two weeks in March by three of the magazine's Singaporean staff.

They dropped documents, bought various items from shops and barged into closing doors in about 10 locations, including Raffles Place, UOB Plaza, Holland Village and Eastpoint shopping centre in Simei.

During rush hour and off-peak times, among young and old, male and female, the findings of their 'unscientific study' were disappointing.

One of the surveyors, associate editor Miss Siti Rohani, 29, said: 'When I dropped my papers in the Citilink Mall, everyone who saw me ignored me. They pretended not to see me or just stepped aside and walked on.'

Only 30 per cent of Singaporeans helped pick up the papers, and only a quarter held doors open for other people.

Most Asian cities fared poorly, with only the citizens of Manila (21st on the survey), Hong Kong and Bangkok (25th), and Jakarta and Taipei (28th), faring slightly better in the courtesy stakes.

The head of the Singapore Kindness Movement (SKM), Mr Noel Hon, was surprised by some of the survey's findings, but said cultivating courtesy was an ongoing, long-term goal.

'We are improving', he said, noting that queuing, a practice once uncommon here, is now standard practice throughout Singapore.

But he acknowledged that 'Singaporeans do need to be reminded to be more courteous, and we will continuously reinforce the message for it to take root'.

The findings come two months before Singapore hosts its largest international event so far, the annual International Monetary Fund and World Bank meetings, to be attended by about 16 000 delegates and visitors.

The Singapore 2006 committee, which is overseeing the event, launched the Four Million Smiles campaign earlier this month, with Prime Minister Lee Hsien Loong saying he wants Singaporeans to give a beaming welcome to the visitors.

To ensure top-notch service, a spokesman for the committee said 21 000 front line service staff would attend a two-day *customer service training* programme.

Training plan misses the target; Costly compulsory course can't teach as well as field visits, job-specific classes
Letter from Nurwati Abd Razak
8 June 2006
TODAY (Singapore)
© 2006. MediaCorp Press Ltd.

I think it is a waste for the Government to spend $4.4 million on the Singapore 2006 *Customer Service Training* programme. It allows taxi drivers or hotel staff to learn more about Singapore and how to promote it. Human resources at the hotel I formerly worked at was naturally happy to make it compulsory for every staff member to attend the course.

Working in the tourism industry, I am always one of the first to know of, be invited to or go for the opening of any new restaurant, pub, club, show, concert or attraction. But what people don't know is that most of the time, we cough up our own money to attend the new attractions and gain in-depth knowledge about them.

It burns a really big hole in our pockets, but what to do?

Rather than look like a stupid fool when guests ask about them (which 10 out of every 10 guests will do), it's better to be well-versed in product knowledge.

Why not have the Singapore Tourism Board produce a special entry pass for customer service personnel – concierges, doormen, front-desk people at shopping malls, restaurants or hotels and, most importantly, customer service officers at tourist attractions – to give them a discount to visit such places? And include discounts on courses, for example, to learn an extra language such as basic Mandarin, Tamil, Japanese, Italian, French or Arabic? Or self-improvement courses on how to deal with a difficult (or, as we call it in the service industry, 'challenging') guest, anger management classes, and so on?

During my last two days tending the concierge desk at my former hotel, which is a five-star hotel famous for its standards and excellent service, I was asked by two foreign guests and a local one how I could keep on smiling and looking happy while running errands for guests from morning to night.

My reply tumbled out without thinking. I said I loved my job of serving people. While I am no bootlicker and can be a very direct person, I get a kick out of helping people. In the end, I benefit from getting exposed to and learning about different cultural behaviours.

This may sound cheesy, but it comes from the bottom of my heart.

If the service personnel the Government is spending taxpayers' money to train are truly passionate, proud and driven in what they do, then they do not need the Government's intervention to insist on compulsory courses to attend.

Simple help with the basic necessities would be enough.

Questions

1 Discuss the concept of politeness as a cultural construct by comparing greetings, thank you's and queuing practices around the world, in small and big cities.

2 If you were running the two-day programme, what approach would you take?

3 Discuss Nurwati Abd Razak's views about spending more on language development and tourism industry knowledge.

References

Argyris, C. (1993) Education for leading-learning. *Organisational Dynamics*, **21**(3).

Berry, L. and Clark, T. (1980) Four ways to make services more tangible. *Business*, **30**, 53–54.

Bove, L. and Johnson, L. (2000) A customer-service worker relationship model. *International Journal of Service Industry Management*, **11**(5), 491–511.

Herzberg, F. (1959) *The motivation to work*. Wiley, New York.

Levesque, P. (2006) *4 steps to spectacular customer service*, viewed 22 May <http://www.entrepreneur.com/article/0,4621,327131,00.html>

Lovelock, C.H. and Wirtz, J. (2004) *Services marketing: people, technology, strategy*, 5th edn. Pearson/Prentice Hall, Upper Saddle River.

McColl-Kennedy, A. and White, T. (1997) Service provider training programs at odds with customer requirements in five star hotels. *Journal of Services Marketing*, **11**(4), 249–264.

Nankervis, A. (2005a) *Managing services*. Cambridge University Press, New York.

Nankervis, A.R. (2005b) *Managing services*. Cambridge University Press, Cambridge, Port Melbourne.

Nankervis, A.R., Compton, R.L. and Baird, M. (2002) *Strategic human resource management*, 4th edn. Nelson, South Melbourne.

Nankervis, A., Compton, R. and Baird, M. (2005) *Human resource management: strategies and processes*, 5th edn. Thomson, Southbank.

Osawa, T. and Ball, S. (2003) The provision of hotel services to international tourists: an investigation of Japanese tourists visiting London hotels. *Journal of Hospitality and Tourism Management*, **10**(20), 196.

Parasuraman, A., Zeithaml, V. and Berry, L. (1998) SERVQUAL. *Journal of Retailing*, **64**, 12–40.

Robbins, S. (2004) *Essentials of organizational behavior*, International Edition, 8th edn. Prentice Hall, Upper Saddle River.

Stevenson, J.C. (2003) *Developing vocational expertise: principles and issues in vocational education*. Allen & Unwin, Crows Nest.

Sturdy, A. (2000) Training in service – importing and imparting customer service culture as an interactive process. *Journal of Human Resource Management*, **11**(6) 1082–1103.

Sureschchandar, G., Chandrasekharan, R. and Kamalanabhan, T. (2001) Customer perceptions of service quality: a critique. *Total Quality Management*, **12**(1), 111–124.

Tsai, M. (2004) Dimensions of Chinese culture values in relation to hotel dining experience. *Journal of Hospitality and Tourism Management*, **11**(1), 13(15).

Zeithaml, V.A., Berry, L.L. and Parasuraman, A. (1991) *The nature and determinants of customer expectations of service.* Marketing Science Institute, Cambridge.

Zeithaml, V.A., Parasuraman, A. and Berry, L.L. (1990) *Delivering quality service: balancing customer perceptions and expectations.* Free Press, Collier Macmillan, New York.

3

Emotional Intelligence

Sensing what others feel without their saying so captures the essence of empathy. Others rarely tell us in words what they feel; instead they tell us in their tone of voice, facial expression, or other non-verbal ways. The ability to sense these subtle communications builds on more basic competencies, particularly self-awareness and self-control. Without the ability to sense our own feelings – or to keep them from swamping us – we will be hopelessly out of touch with the moods of others.

Goleman, 1998, p. 135

Central theme

Customer service has a significant affective component. Employees need to be able to recognize and regulate their emotions and manage the customer service interaction on an emotional level by recognizing the emotional needs and wants of others.

Training implications

1 Explain the mission and values of the organization in terms of the emotional dimension of customer service. This will differ markedly, for example, from pizza shop to doctor's surgery.

2 Use the wealth of life experience of adult learners as the starting point for training.

3 When reflecting on service, or analysing scenarios, encourage learners to:
   - listen to their emotions and those of the customer
   - ask the right questions
   - use multiple perceptions
   - work out appropriate solutions
   - align responses with the organization's values
   - manage emotions, self and customer
   - use abilities cross-contextually, transferring learning from one situation to the next
   - model excellence in others
   - resolve problems and conflicts
   - work congruently and in harmony with others.

4 Use reflective practices to ask, 'What happened?', 'What would I do differently?' and 'What would I do the same?'

Introduction

The construct of emotional intelligence (EI) is closely linked to the notion of attitude, heard about so frequently when a trainer bemoans the quality of service personnel: 'They have such a bad attitude these days!' Salovey and Mayer (1990) were the first to adopt the terminology 'emotional intelligence' and expand on earlier work by Gardner (1983) on interpersonal and intrapersonal intelligence. More recently, Goleman (1995) has extended this work into the business arena, popularizing the idea that emotional intelligence is as important, if not more important, than IQ. The five areas of emotional intelligence are:

- knowing your emotions (recognizing one's own feelings, self-awareness)

- regulating your emotions (handling feelings, bouncing back)

- being able to motivate yourself (emotional control, self-motivation and creativity)

- recognizing emotions in others (empathy, being attuned to emotional signals from others)

- handling relationships (managing emotions in others, social competence).

These authors describe emotional intelligence as skill in the *affective* domain. For years psychologists and educators have discussed three domains: the affective domain (emotions); the psychomotor domain (behaviours); and the cognitive domain (thinking). Indeed, Bloom (1956) developed a taxonomy of learning in which the affective domain included receiving phenomena, responding to phenomena, valuing phenomena and organizing phenomena. We will return to this taxonomy again when looking at behaviour modification approaches in Chapter Four and cognitive processes in the development of expertise in Chapter Seven. However, it must be pointed out at this stage that these domains overlap. Goleman (1995) points out that emotional intelligence competencies combine both cognitive and emotional skills. This author takes the position that EI should prove a more powerful predictor of success than IQ within a job or profession. In this context, leading edge researchers in the Emotional

Intelligence Consortium at Rutgers University (Druskat et al., 2005) have recently put forward convincing cases for the strong link between EI and workplace performance. There is, however, much debate about the capacity of EI tests as predictors of workplace performance and there are many research projects that have looked at the reliability and validity of predictive tests, the findings of which are inconclusive (Davies et al., 1998; Dulewicz and Higgs, 1998).

For the moment, however, a trainer can readily see the value of developing emotional sensitivity, a higher level of awareness of the emotions of others and an ability to regulate one's own emotions. Sensitivity to the emotions of others is particularly relevant when establishing customer needs. First, there is the quiet customer who has a problem but is too nervous to bring it to someone's attention. Then there is the customer who shouts: 'These people are thieves, watch the consumer show on television tonight, they are ripping you off!' Clearly, an employee who is able to sense the first complaint and resolve the second before the customer explodes would be highly valued.

More recently, Merlevede et al. (2000) have extended the general concept of emotional intelligence to include a number of specific components, namely:

- listening to your emotions for their message value

- asking the right questions and using multiple perceptions

- creatively working out appropriate solutions

- aligning responses with higher meta-levels of identity, mission etc.

- managing emotions to achieve goals

- using abilities cross-contextually

- using examples of excellence in others as models of practice

- resolving conflicts

- living congruently in harmony with self and others.

Of these, the concept of using abilities cross-contextually relates to skill transfer from one service occupation to another.

When hiring and training a new employee, the manager's purpose is to build on social skills already developed in other contexts and apply them in the current context where the customers are different, the product is different and the consumer decision-making process is weighted higher or lower in importance (usually related to the total cost of the product or its perceived value).

Implications for employee selection

Before discussing training implications of the concept of emotional intelligence, let us deal briefly with employee selection. Most employers will agree that attitudes and values are well established before the employee is hired and are somewhat resilient to change: 'Once a bad attitude, always a bad attitude.' While behaviourists will present a different argument in the next chapter, this is largely true. The question is: 'How can selection procedures best predict the service provider's responses in customer interactions?'

Current proponents of EI suggest that tests such as the Emotional Competency Inventory can be used as selection tools to assist with better decision-making about recruitment. The type of question the candidate would be asked to rate themselves on would be similar to the following:

Example 1

I attempt to find common ground in situations where I face disagreement with others.
   Never   Seldom   Sometimes   Usually   Always

Example 2

I balance thoughts and feelings when making decisions.
   Never   Seldom   Sometimes   Usually   Always

Example 3

I prefer to reflect before beginning a task.
   Never   Seldom   Sometimes   Usually   Always
   Source: http://www.ase-solutions.co.uk/index.asp

There are many such self-rating screening tests and it is essential to look at the reliability and validity of these measurement instruments (Gable and Wolf, 1993). In some cases, the authors have gone to great lengths to study predictive validity over a long period. Can a test such as this predict the emotional intelligence of a new employee? Will a high level of emotional intelligence be reflected in job performance? Are different job environments, such as nursing and hairdressing, so different that these social skills are more or less appropriate? Are they required in different measures at different times?

The tests described here involve self-assessment. In employee recruitment, one of the current trends is to use *behavioural interviewing* in order to improve selection decisions. Thus, for the first self-assessment question described earlier, the interviewer would ask, 'Can you describe a situation in which you faced a disagreement with a customer?' Probing questions would establish the approach taken by the applicant to resolve the conflict. It can be argued that, once again, the applicant would tailor the answer to the expectations of the interviewer. However, it is much more difficult to create a fake customer conflict than it is to rate oneself on a self-evident rating scale where you 'usually' or 'always' find 'common ground' with others.

Some of the questions that could be asked in an interview include:

- Can you describe any imaginative solution that you have found to a customer's problem?

- How did you sense that the customer had a problem?

- Do you have an example of a work situation in which you paused to reflect (think about your course of action) beforehand?

- How did you feel after that?

In practice

Rank the following occupations in order of the importance of emotional intelligence to competent job performance:

- Hairdresser
- Consultant
- Salesperson
- Banquet attendant

- Veterinarian

- Nurse

- Teacher

- Internet service provider

- Investment analyst

Discuss the question: Is the 'emotional intelligence' required the same in all cases despite the different level of importance for each occupation? In other words is the construct (concept) of emotional intelligence the same in all cases or different?

Attitudinal training

As a trainer, can you influence attitudes and emotions? Can you lead employees to the sincere belief that 'the customer is king'? Can you coach employees to be more responsive to the emotional environment in which they work, with both their colleagues and their customers?

If we take the list of emotional intelligence competencies developed by Merlevede et al. (2000) described earlier, we can look at training strategies to enhance the development of emotional literacy from a number of viewpoints.

Listening to your emotions for their message value

Here the trainee is asked to pay attention to their emotional response to a customer service situation. This could be a reflection on a previous experience or a response to a scenario or role play. For example, the customer is highly emotional or possibly under the influence of drugs or alcohol; the child is throwing a tantrum because they want their fries longer and thinner; the customer is complaining because the haircut is shorter than expected; the patient is confused and distressed. In these situations, you are asking the trainee about how the customer might feel (empathy) as well as how they feel themselves. In some cases, the emotional labour of a job (staying upbeat all the time or dealing with stress and sadness) needs to be considered carefully, including the flow-on effects of this emotion to other customers and to fellow employees.

Asking the right questions and using multiple perceptions

Here the trainer is asking the employee to become more attentive to customer cues. What are the signals that the customer needs attention; what are the signals that the answers provided are not relevant or helpful; and what are the signals that the customer is likely to take the complaint to a higher level? The right questions are open ended and not closed (yes/no answers). Active listening skills are used to explore issues and perceptions on both sides of the service interaction.

Creatively working out appropriate solutions

Workplace policies and procedures are usually constraints when trying to reach creative solutions. Here the trainer would take a sample policy, such as returns and refunds, and look at how these may be interpreted, or indeed breached. In some organizations, employees are empowered to make decisions such as these up to a maximum monetary value (for example, 'You can spend up to $200 a week to keep customers happy, no questions asked').

Aligning responses with higher meta-levels of identity, mission etc.

This is linked to the previous element where policies and procedures emerge from an organizational mission statement or purpose. The trainee might be provided with ethically complex decisions and be encouraged to use frameworks for evaluating responses to these ethical dilemmas (large and small) that might occur in the workplace (for example, customers stealing glassware; faded signatures on credit cards; desire to enter sites outside permitted hours; access to closed areas; upgrading to better seats; favours for preferred clients).

Managing emotions to achieve goals

In many of the helping professions, it is necessary to sublimate emotions during times of crisis, such as medical emergency responses. In others, fraught emotions can emerge in hot and busy work environments such as kitchens.

Working in close proximity, working with limited, shared resources, and working to unrealistic deadlines all impact on the employee's capacity to achieve customer service goals. These scenarios can provide for fruitful analysis in training sessions.

Using abilities cross-contextually

The adult learner brings a life of experience to the college or workplace. These can be explored to see how social skills are applied:

- What happened and why?
- What would you do differently if you did it again?
- What would you do the same if you did it again?
- How is this relevant to the scenario we are discussing?

These questions are powerful training tools. They ask the learner to reflect and analyse, to make connections and see relevance.

Modelling excellence in others

Identifying positive attributes and service excellence in others is another way to develop emotional intelligence. This can be done by watching the skilled customer relations performance of others. However, one needs to do more than just watch; the performance needs to be articulated and analysed for its success factors:

- What did he/she do?
- How did the customer respond?
- What would you do differently?
- What would you do the same?

This approach, followed by the opportunity to apply learning immediately with consequent rewards is likely to establish high levels of performance (providing that this level is perceived as achievable).

In practice

Fake abuse for bus drivers
From: *Daily Telegraph*
June 27, 2006

It's the job everyone is qualified for. State Transit is going to pay people to give government bus drivers a verbal pummelling. Actors and frequent bus travellers are being hired to pose as irate customers in the taxpayer-funded project. In a twist on patrons paying for being late or left on the side of the road, successful applicants will get $23.16 an hour to vent their spleen and prepare drivers for the public relations warfare they face on the streets. But trainers really need not go further than their local bus stop. John Braver of Hillsdale said bus drivers are 'uncourteous'. 'I've seen them take off with elderly passengers stumbling over their grocery bags in the aisle,' he said.

Matraville resident Heidi Schobel, 23, said the Government should listen to the public before wasting money hiring actors, while Luis Flores from Randwick said more buses are needed in the mornings.

http://www.news.com.au/story/0,10117,19601883-13762,00.html

Questions

1 Prepare to discuss the general issues raised by this article.

2 As a trainer, develop scripts for two actors acting as abusive bus commuters.

3 As a trainer, develop guidelines for customer service for the trainee bus drivers.

4 Identify policies and procedures for handling emotionally charged incidents ranging from minor to major (where police are called and assault charges are laid – either party, the driver or commuter!).

5 Having prepared trainees by discussing the issues, policies and their own experiences in similar contexts, ask them to role play the two incidents allowing them to develop or escalate in different and imaginative ways.

6 Working with the trainees, review the role plays in an open way discussing the emotions involved and 'what would you do differently?' and 'what would you do the same?'

7 Finally, consolidate the learning by discussing the trainee's conclusions followed by a 'best result' role play scripted by the trainees and acted out. As the trainer, do not hesitate to become involved as an actor at any stage. The collaborative outcome is at best partial as not every scenario can be anticipated. The aim is to cover multiple perspectives and allow creativity in finding alternatives.

Resolving conflicts

In customer service books, writers always refer to problems as conflicts. More often than not, the customer has a problem that requires resolution and it is not a conflict. For example, 'My hotel room is not made up. I know that check in is 2 pm but I have been flying for 24 hours and my baby is crying'; 'The hot water in my room is cold'; 'This product does not work'; 'This is not what I expected from the brochure'. When the trainee is able to differentiate between a problem and a conflict, to show empathy, to find creative solutions, to work within policy guidelines and to resolve or report real conflicts, then they have reached a higher level of emotional intelligence as defined by the writers in this field.

Living congruently in harmony with self and others

Attention to the values of the workplace is an essential element of training. There may be conflicting values held by informal groups. These need to be discussed. Laziness, lack of productivity, sabotage and other negative behaviours may be exhibited by self or others. This is another challenge for the trainer who must be aware of attribution theory (Weiner, 2005). When errors occur, judgments of responsibility vary from internal causation (I was lazy, not careful enough) to external causation (it was bad luck, bad management by someone else).

When debriefing after hectic service periods, the manager must be mindful of attribution error. Review of what went well, and what did not go well, needs to be carefully analysed by asking all participants to reflect on the question, 'Why?' Finally, returning to the concept of emotional intelligence, Goleman (1996) suggests that trainers ought to develop emotional literacy by asking learners to be more attentive to emotions, including their own and others'. Questions can be asked, such as:

- How did you feel?

- How did you manage your feelings?

- How did the customer respond emotionally?

- How did you manage the interpersonal relationship on an emotional level?

The last of these questions refers to the service provider's capacity to establish the emotional tone of the interaction. It could be positive and upbeat, or a conflict situation could be resolved leading to quiet satisfaction on the part of the customer.

Turning awareness into competence

While it is all very well to raise an individual's awareness of his or her own and others' emotions, this in turn needs to lead to change in action. For example, an individual responding to some of the questions asked in this chapter may be able to conceptualize different perspectives and resolutions to situations. However, the steps that follow involve practicing new skills and dealing with new outcomes. For new behaviours to become part of an individual's repertoire, these responses need to be tried, tested and evaluated. In the next chapter, we will look at the ways in which outcomes influence behaviour.

Summary

The construct of emotional intelligence assists trainers in formulating training approaches that place emotional factors at the forefront of training design. The aim is to develop employees who are more attentive to their emotional responses and those of their customers and more appropriately responsive in a range of situations.

While pre-employment screening tests for positive service personality traits appear to offer limited assistance to employers, behavioural interviewing techniques can improve the quality of selection outcomes. This chapter focuses on a much neglected element of customer service training, that of emotional literacy. By highlighting this aspect of the customer service encounter, trainers can develop skills in active listening, empathy and ability to manage emotions, of self and others.

On reflection

Correctional services

In our facility Correctional Services Officers (CSRs) should be able to:

- Conduct interactions with offenders in a fair, just, humane and positive manner

- Use communication strategies with individuals for effective interaction and problem solving

- Consider cultural sensitivities in communication techniques and adapt style and language to accommodate different cultural values and practices

- Identify potential causes of conflict and use a range of appropriate and effective defusing responses

Questions

1 Discuss the concept of prisoners as customers in the correctional service system.

2 Give your views on the potential use of service orientation or emotional intelligence personality tests for selecting staff for correctional service roles.

3 Describe the organizational culture of a correctional service facility (there are some websites with mission/vision statements).

4 As a trainer of correctional service officers, explain how the construct of emotional intelligence can be used to support a training initiative which develops the skills listed earlier.

References

Bloom, B.S. (1956) *Taxonomy of educational objectives.* Longmans Green, New York.

Davies, M., Stankov, L. and Roberts, R. (1998) Emotional intelligence: in search of an elusive construct. *Journal of Personality and Social Psychology*, 75(4), 989–1015.

Druskat, V.U., Sala, F. and Mount, G.J. (eds) (2005) *Linking emotional intelligence and performance at work.* Jossey-Bass, San Francisco.

Dulewicz, V. and Higgs, M. (1998) Emotional intelligence: can it be measured reliably and validly using competency data? *Competency*, 6(1).

Gable, R.K. and Wolf, M.B. (1993) *Instrument development in the affective domain: measuring attitudes and values in corporate and school settings*, 2nd edn. Kluwer Academic Press, Boston.

Gardner, H. (1983) *Frames of mind: the theory of multiple intelligences*, 10th anniversary edn. Basic Books, New York.

Goleman, D. (1995) *The emotionally intelligent workplace.* Bantam Books, New York.

Goleman, D. (1996) *Emotional intelligence.* Bloomsbury Publishing, London.

Goleman, D. (1998) *Working with emotional intelligence.* Bantam Books, New York.

Merlevede, P., Bridoux, D. and Vandamme, R. (2000) *7 Steps to emotional intelligence.* Crown House Publications, Bancyfelin.

Salovey, P. and Mayer, J. (1990) Emotional intelligence. *Imagination, Cognition and Personality*, 9, 185–211.

Weiner, B. (2005) Motivation from an attribution perspective and the social psychology of perceived competence. In *Handbook of competence and motivation* (A. Elliot and C. Dweck, eds). Guilford Press, New York.

4

Reinforcement Theory

Learning is an enduring change in the mechanisms of behaviour involving specific stimuli and/or responses that result from prior experience with those or similar stimuli and responses...The only way to prove that the training experience is causing the behaviour change of interest is to experimentally vary the presence and absence of that experience. For this reason, learning can be investigated only with experimentation techniques.

Domjan, 2003, p. 15

Central theme

Behaviour modification principles can be used to shape effective customer service behaviours. Reinforcement can occur in the form of extrinsic rewards provided by customers, supervisors or peers. Alternatively, reinforcement can occur in the form of self-reinforcement (intrinsic reward). Intermittent reinforcement creates the most sustainable behaviour. Performance standards (verbal coding of exemplary customer service behaviours) can contribute to the individual's capacity for self-reinforcement.

Training implications

1 Describe learning outcomes in behavioural terms.

2 Use tangible and intangible rewards for reinforcement.

3 Use observational learning to build performance to the required standard.

4 While shaping behaviour ensure that each level of performance is achievable.

5 Explain and demonstrate what exemplary customer service looks like so that learners can become self-reinforcing when they achieve the performance standard.

6 Consolidate behaviour and transfer across a range of scenarios.

Introduction

Training plans usually have behavioural outcomes or objectives as the focal point. This is not to say that affective and cognitive outcomes are not achieved too, as these three domains seldom work in isolation. However, most trainers have been taught to respond to the question, 'what will the trainee be able to do on completion of the training?' These learning objectives usually commence with an action beginning. For example, on completion of training, the trainee will be able to:

- greet the customer courteously

- establish the customer's needs

- assist with product decision-making

- close the sale

- process payment.

Whereas in the previous chapter the focus was primarily on the antecedents of behaviour, the 'emotional intelligence' and other capabilities that the candidate brought to the training situation, this approach to training has *outcomes* as the focus. Here the trainer is establishing behaviour expressed as an outcome of training and occurring as a result of positive reinforcement. This is where the notion of operant conditioning provides an additional perspective for the trainer to design ways in which they can improve training effectiveness.

The psychologist, B. F. Skinner (1953) suggests that an individual's actions are a result of the consequences that have followed previous behaviours. Where similar behaviour has been reinforced, it will be repeated. In the training situation, the desired behaviour is demonstrated as part of the practice session, reinforced if correctly performed, and perhaps fine tuned before being reinforced again. Reinforcement can come in many forms, both tangible and intangible, short term and long term, internal and external:

- praise

- attention

- course completion

- certification

- self-assessment checklist

- sense of achievement

■ acknowledgement of cause and effect (e.g. customer satisfaction, thanks, more sales, more commission, more tips!)

■ personal development, self-actualization

■ peer support.

Simply expressed, this theory suggests that behaviour is shaped by contingent consequences. Behaviour that is reinforced is more likely to be exhibited again; behaviour that is punished is less likely to be exhibited again; and behaviour that fails to lead to any consequence is likely to be extinguished. This, of course, assumes a highly rational view of behaviour.

Determining a training need

In organizational development terms, a 'training need' refers to a deficiency in performance. It is a gap between what the employee can do and needs to do. However, too often, this performance deficiency is not a training need at all. A diagram can be used to illustrate this in a simple way. As Figure 4.1 shows, the first task is to describe the behaviour deficiency. One also needs to analyse the reasons for non-performance. For example, a help desk employee may be asked to respond to e-mails from new customers within a half-hour period. Instead, the employee is found searching the Internet for holiday information, leaving the e-mails for responses by other staff. The first question to be asked is whether there is indeed a skill deficiency. Does the employee know how to respond to e-mails, does s/he know about the half-hour rule? If it is not a skill deficiency, it is not a training need but instead a motivational or performance management issue. When analysing the reasons for non-performance, there are many possibilities. There may be obstacles, such as temporary intranet downtime. Alternatively, the employee may be on the verge of resigning to move cities. There may also be replacement (inappropriate) behaviours that are more rewarding, in this case surfing the Internet looking for holiday information. Finally, one must ask, 'is the desired behaviour punished?' This may sound absurd until one looks at the help desk employee's behaviour in the context of a company policy. This policy, which says to the customer, 'your *first* contact with us will be your *final* contact – we are a one stop customer help shop', may shed new light on this problem. In this organization, the employee who picks up a new help desk question is totally responsible for that customer and continues to work with the customer until the issue is resolved. Thus, by picking up too many 'first question' help desk calls, the employee may build a workload beyond their perceived capacity. Since each new customer is an extra burden, picking up the customer query is punishing. This needs to be resolved by management systems dealing with policy, work load and measures of performance.

Let us return to the skill deficiency question: if it is a skill deficiency, then the employee needs training, reinforcement, practice and consolidation to develop

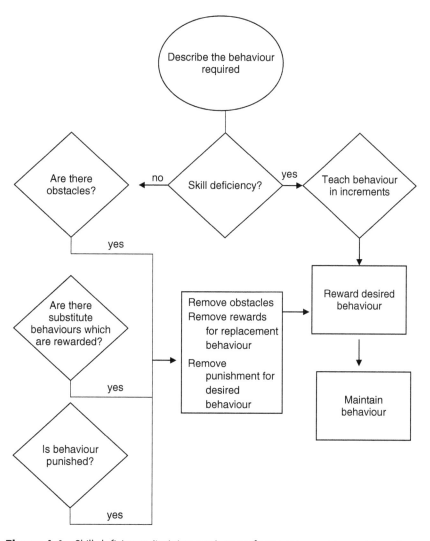

Figure 4.1 Skill deficiency (training gap) or performance management issue?

the skill to an optimal level. Finally, the trained behaviour needs to be maintained with attention to intermittent reinforcement and a watchful brief on the performance management issues described earlier that could arise.

This theoretical approach highlights the importance of practice, repetition and reinforcement in training, the four familiar training steps being 'tell, show, do, review'. One-sided training, where the trainee is not given an opportunity to consolidate behaviour, is valueless. Anyone who has watched a computer demonstration without the opportunity for immediate and repeated application would know this!

Another concept provided by behavioural theorists is that of shaping. Here, the trainer assists the trainee to reach the required performance outcomes by developing skills slowly, with goals and targets to set achievement levels during the shaping process. If these levels are set too high, there is the risk that the trainee will fail and lose motivation. This is a form of failure in front of peers which, in this framework, is defined as punishment. The trainer's skill is to develop and reinforce successive approximations of the final behaviour until the final, desired outcome is achieved.

Supervisors and managers shape employee behaviour every day by applying and withdrawing reinforcement or rewards, often unintentionally. Nods, smiles, pats on the back and words of encouragement are all forms of positive reinforcement. Unfortunately, the wrong behaviour is often positively reinforced, for example, 'you can't do that, let me do it for you'. Simply taking over and allowing an employee to 'get away with it' is reinforcing laziness. Providing help is sometimes unhelpful!

In practice

Discuss the efficacy of the following approaches to keeping the service area and visible workstations clean and tidy:

1 The agency manager having a tantrum when the place is a mess after a busy service period.

2 Notices in the back office appealing to everyone's better nature.

3 Demerit points allocated after routine inspections.

4 A cleaning roster.

5 An occasional lottery ticket for staff members maintaining a tidy workspace.

6 A plastic dollop from the joke shop assigned to the most untidy staff member of the week.

7 Office re-design to include better storage.

8 A patronizing pat on the back from the agency manager.

Do you have any other ideas?

Reinforcement schedules

Many scientific studies of reinforcement schedules have demonstrated that intermittent reinforcement is more effective than constant reinforcement (Skinner, 1953; Bandura, 1969). Poker machine players demonstrate that gambling behaviour can be well maintained by intermittent rewards, either at variable intervals of time or amounts of payout. There is no need to reward every performance in order to consolidate the behaviour. In fact, research has shown that varying the schedule of reinforcement will establish a behaviour very strongly after it has been initially learned. As time goes by the intervals between reinforcement can grow wider and wider. Extinction (elimination) only occurs a long interval after the last reinforcement and is very hard to achieve when behaviour, such as gambling, is well established. In the workplace, the undesired behaviours are, for example, those that avoid work, and those that enable the individual to avoid being detected. The individual may have been rewarded for these avoidance behaviours for some time and this is termed negative reinforcement.

> Evidence of schedule control of behaviour has important implications for the understanding of behaviour and its modification. Those who have been reared under more or less continuous reinforcement conditioning are likely to become easily discouraged and cease responding when faced with frustrating non-reward or failure. By contrast, persons whose response patterns have been reinforced only intermittently will persist in their behaviour for a considerable time despite setbacks and infrequent reinforcement (Bandura, 1969, p. 29).

Articulating outcomes

The challenge for trainers in the area of customer service is the difficulty associated with articulating or demonstrating the behaviours expected. This is easy when psychomotor skills are involved, such as taking a food order, but much more difficult when describing communication with the customer. In Table 4.1, the judging criteria for restaurant service awards are described. The behaviours are categorized and described, and readers should take particular note of the highest level service descriptor in each category. These are known as BARS, behaviourally anchored rating scales. These are helpful in that an employee with a 'bad attitude' can be led to a better understanding of what a 'good attitude' looks and sounds like. For example, behaviours demonstrated by waiting staff can range from 'unresponsive to customers' questions and requests for information' through to 'level of connectedness and conversational engagement is ideal for the style of establishment and mood of guests'.

This table can be used by the organization to drive training. Employees can be judged by peers, by mystery customers, by real customers and by real judges. The provision of corrective feedback and reinforcement of desired behaviours can establish a solid repertoire. One additional way in which this type of behavioural scale can be used is for a self-rating. Role plays and video taped episodes can also be used to measure against this type of scale.

Benefits of reinforcement

There are many benefits associated with using reinforcement as a training tool. Not only is behaviour established and consolidated:

- there is a flow on motivational affect across all skill sets

- once established by intermittent reinforcement, the behaviour will continue in the absence of the trainer

Table 4.1 Service dimensions for restaurant judging

Criteria	Pointers
Staff presentation Cleanliness, consistency, stylishness, polish in personal presentation, including contemporary non-matching uniforms where appropriate	■ poor personal hygiene or cleanliness, e.g. dirty hair, nails ■ uniforms unacceptable or absent ■ staff presentation barely acceptable ■ mostly well presented and appropriate to style and décor ■ consistent high quality personal presentation, polish and style, enhances service and ambience
Verbal communication and voice quality Language used appropriate, clear and easy to understand. Tone of voice and volume. Appropriate to style of restaurant and clientele. Multi-language skills	■ customer unable to hear or understand staff or make him/herself understood ■ barely able to understand staff ■ communication sufficient to get by and order ■ volume, tone and articulation ideal for context, language used appropriately ■ verbal communication ability contributes in a positive way to dining experience
Non-verbal communication Attentive non-verbal communication. Responding to eye-contact, smiles. Posture appropriate	■ signs of boredom, suppressed anger or frustration, deliberately ignoring customers ■ general lack of attention, signs of stress ■ generally acceptable non-verbal communication ■ appropriate non-verbal gestures, posture and attentive response ■ positive non-verbal communication enhances service experience through attentiveness, enthusiasm, friendliness or discretion expressed non-verbally and where appropriate

(Continued)

Table 4.1 (Continued)

Criteria	Pointers
Conversation and connection with guests Ability to gauge customer's desire for small talk, responding appropriately, asking questions and providing information (e.g. local attractions)	■ unresponsive to questions, does not provide requested information ■ inaccurate assessment of mood of table ■ generally acceptable responses to guest-initiated conversation or questions ■ appropriate topics discussed, interest taken in customers and information needs met ■ level of connectedness and conversational engagement ideal for the style of establishment and mood of guests
Knowledge and explanation of menu and wine list Able to describe in detail the menu ingredients and cooking methods. Able to describe and discuss wines and assist with guest selection. Able to provide information and assistance on special dietary needs including relevant menu or special dish dietary information	■ unable to understand and answer questions about menu or wine list ■ able to re-iterate information already provided on menus and wine lists ■ can describe and discuss menu/wine list items including ingredients and preparation ■ accurate advice in the area of special dietary needs/menu or wine selection displaying detailed enterprise knowledge ■ exemplary explanations demonstrating in-depth industry product knowledge in all features and professional sales technique
Teamwork Evidence of teamwork, collaboration and positive interaction between staff members	■ evidence of tension between team members ■ team members serve only allocated customers and do not assist one another

- generally comfortable working relationships evident
- positive teamwork evident in body language and verbal communication with colleagues
- dynamic synergy between team members contributes in a positive way to the customer experience

Judgment and contingency response

Able to exhibit judgment and superior problem-solving skills. Shows initiative in responding to guests' unexpressed needs

- does not perceive customer needs, absent from area
- unresponsive to customer's attempt to seek assistance
- provides minimal response and limited assistance in problem-solving
- perceptive, helpful and positive attitude towards finding solutions
- outstanding judgment in relation to problem expressed and solution provided, going beyond normal expectations for contingency response

Response to unusual requests

Receptive to requests such as non-standard items, unusual food combinations, moving seating etc.

- unwilling to consider special request, flat 'no', dismissive
- listens attentively to special request but does not act on it, apologizes
- takes action to process special request but seems somewhat reluctant
- listens and understands request and provides alternatives and solutions
- responds promptly and positively, makes an immediate and unqualified effort to meet the request

(Continued)

Table 4.1 (Continued)

Criteria	Pointers
Feedback, finalization and farewell Attempts of staff to check satisfaction, process money efficiently and farewell customers expressing a genuine attempt to provide current and future service	■ slow processing of finalization, no farewell or feedback sought at any time ■ efficient but unfriendly finalization ■ feedback sought from customers (closed question) and standard finalization routine and farewell ■ active feedback sought from customer, efficient processing and friendly farewell ■ feedback, finalization and genuine farewell used to demonstrate the value of the customer in the present and in the future

© M Van Der Wagen

- intrinsic rewards (internally provided, not external) become more powerful

- positive behaviours lead to other outcomes, such as customer satisfaction which in itself becomes rewarding

- self-esteem grows

- the learner is motivated to learn more.

It must be noted that customer service is not a largely psychomotor activity like roof tiling, sawing, drilling etc. It requires knowledge acquisition (who are our customers?) and cognitive processing (when is this behaviour appropriate?). An employee is not simply trained to be friendly. Different levels of friendliness are needed for children, regular customers and customers from other cultures who may take offence if not treated formally. Friendliness and good humor can be regarded as inappropriate by some. This is where we fall back on conceptions such as emotional intelligence and acknowledge the complexity of this field of interpersonal communication.

In practice

Develop a series of training objectives linked to appropriate service contexts using five of the following adverbs (or equivalent verbs):
 welcoming; gracious; forthcoming; responsive; sociable; pleasant; gregarious; outgoing; convivial; affable.

Application of behaviour management in the workplace

A study conducted in police stations to measure improvement in customer service behaviours through organizational behaviour management showed that performance improvements were achieved through reinforcement interventions and were maintained over time (Boni and Wilson, 1994). First, public perceptions were measured to determine the behaviours necessary to ensure satisfactory service and to ascertain the importance of these behaviours. The target behaviours identified by the public are shown in Table 4.2.

Table 4.2 The target behaviours identified by the public

Target behaviour description phrase	Target behaviour reference
Attending to the customer promptly	Promptness
Friendly tone of voice	Voice tone
Attending to one customer at a time	Undivided attention
Giving the customer full attention by use of eye-contact, nods and comments such as 'OK'	Attentiveness
Smiling or a friendly expression	Smiling
Providing an appropriate greeting	Greeting/offering to assist
Ending the exchange appropriately	Parting/referral phrase
Offering extra help or information	Extra help
Use of formal, polite terms	Respect

Source: Boni and Wilson, 1994

A workshop was then conducted with the police participants to clarify the public perceptions of satisfactory service identified in the first phase of the research. This led to increases in 'overall courtesy' which was an index of the extent to which the attendant displayed each of the nine target courtesy behaviours. However, most of the sustained performance improvement occurred after a process of reinforcement intervention and corrective feedback. The identification of the expected courtesy behaviours and their ratings by the public were an important part of this study summarized as follows:

Promptness (Value – 22 points)

Promptness was measured as the time it took for an attendant to acknowledge a customer verbally (e.g. 'Good morning') or non-verbally (e.g. a nod of the head). Measurement of time began at entry to the station and ceased at acknowledgement. The actual time interval was measured by the observer with a stopwatch that was hidden from general view. In order to score 22 points for promptness, the attendant was required to acknowledge the customer within 15 seconds of entry to the station, although the officer did not need actually to attend to the enquiry within this time. For example, the offer of a seat, or an acknowledgement that the person would be attended to in due course, was deemed sufficient.

Voice tone (Value – 18 points)

The tone of the attendant's voice was adjudicated by the observer as either acceptable (i.e. normal and non-raised) or unacceptable (i.e. impatient, rude, indifferent, angry, hostile or abrupt). In order to score 18 points, the attendant had to maintain a normal, non-raised voice throughout the entire interaction.

Undivided attention (Value – 14 points)

Observers recorded whether the officer paid attention to the customer throughout the entire interaction. The attendants did not score for this behaviour if they undertook other duties while attending to the customer, if they attended to another customer simultaneously, or if they continued a conversation with a fellow staff member. To score 14 points, the attendant was required to show the customer undivided attention, except when acknowledging the arrival of another customer.

Attentiveness (Value – 14 points)

Attentiveness comprised verbal and non-verbal responses made by attendants while listening to the customer, which indicated that they were paying attention. Acceptable verbal responses included acknowledgements such as 'mm', 'yes', or 'I see', and questioning phrases such as 'really?', 'did you?', or 'oh?'. Non-verbal behaviours of this kind included nodding. To score 14 points, the attendant was required to show at least one of these responses at some stage during the interaction.

Smiling (Value – 13 points)

The officer received 13 points for smiling at either the beginning or end of an interaction, thereby conveying a friendly manner.

Greeting/offering to assist (Value – 12 points)

Officers were scored on the appropriateness of their initial greeting when first attending to the customer. Appropriate greetings included: 'Hello', 'Good day', 'Good morning/afternoon' and 'How are you today?'. Points were also awarded for direct offers of assistance, such as 'May I help you?', 'Have you been attended to?', 'Can I be of some assistance?', or 'Is anyone waiting to be served?' (described as primary assisting phrases). Indirect acknowledgements or offers of assistance (e.g. 'yes') were recorded on the Observation Record Sheet as secondary assisting phrases but did not receive any points. In order to score 12 points for greeting/offering to assist, the attendant had to use any greeting or direct, formal offer of assistance.

Parting/referral phrase (Value – 10 points)

Points were assigned to the officer if he or she used an appropriate formal parting phrase (primary parting phrase) at the end of the interaction. Formal phrases included: 'Have a nice day'; 'Thanks for letting us know'; 'If you have any further problems please let us know'; 'We will do the best we can'; 'X will be with you shortly'; 'Goodbye'; and 'Thanks very much'. Less formal (secondary parting phrases) were recorded on the Observation Record Sheet and were also awarded full points. These included: 'Alright?'; 'No worries mate'; 'OK?'; 'There you go'; and 'No problems'. The attendant did not receive any points if he or she failed to acknowledge verbally the end of the interaction.

Extra help (Value – 10 points)

Points were awarded if the attendant spontaneously offered extra assistance during the interaction. The opportunity to offer such additional assistance, or clarification, did not arise for every enquiry and, indeed, it was not appropriate or relevant for the attendant to offer extra help to every customer (e.g. if a customer entered the station for an appointment or simply to collect an item or document). However, certain enquiries, such as those that involved detailed explanations and requests for directions, provided an opportunity to extend such extra service to customers and, where this service was provided, 10 points were added to the score. Examples of offers of extra help included: 'Is there anything you are unsure about?'; 'Do you have any other questions?'; 'Can I be of any further assistance?'; 'Are you sure you know where to go?'; 'If you are still confused, you can find out more by going to . . .'; 'If we hear anything further about it we'll let you know'; and 'Would you like me to leave them a message?'.

Respect (Value – 10 points)

Points were awarded if the attendant used formal, polite phrases including 'sir' and 'madam'. Other formal phrases for which 10 points were awarded included:

'Excuse me while I make a call'; 'I'm sorry to have kept you waiting'; 'This may take a few minutes. Would you like to take a seat?'.

This type of intervention provides a clear example of behaviour modification principles in practice. In all training circumstances, the question has to be asked, 'do they know how to do it?' Sometimes, hurdles in the form of bottlenecks, procedures and shortage of resources can prevent the desired behaviour being exhibited, in others it may be due to a lack of motivation. The trainer needs to give consideration to the desired outcomes and then analyse the reasons for inadequate performance. If a training need is clearly identified then this approach is a sound one for many workplace contexts.

Modelling

Following the work of Skinner (1953), a world renowned psychologist, Albert Bandura (1969) developed the theory of observational learning. He agreed with Skinner that behaviour can be acquired by conditioning; however, he added that learning can also be acquired by modelling the behaviour of others. Using this approach, the trainer, supervisor or workplace colleague can demonstrate the required performance so that the trainee can model the requisite behaviours. While this sounds very logical in theory, it is surprising how many trainers are not prepared to model best practice. Indeed, they are reluctant to demonstrate any form of practice. Any demonstration, good, average or bad, would provide for fruitful discussions in the training room and a learning experience for all, if it was openly analysed and evaluated. In doing this, the trainer debriefs the group in terms of the experience for the customer, the outcomes for the organization and, most importantly, the emotions, behaviours and decisions exhibited by the training provider.

Bandura also points to extensive research support for the idea that self-reinforcement plays a potentially more important role than external reinforcement in the behaviour of adults. This is done by establishing what worthy performance looks like and by verbally coding steps in its achievement (Bandura and Mischel, 1965). The results of these studies also show that 'people generally adopt the standards for self-reinforcement exhibited by exemplary models, they evaluate their own performance relative to that standard, and then they serve as their own reinforcing agents' (Bandura, 1969, p. 33).

Finally, Bandura points out that people can learn merely by watching. In this way, by observing the behaviour of others and their consequences, adults learn about many different social behaviours. In the customer service environment, service providers can learn by imitating the effective behaviour of colleagues and being rewarded externally or by self-praise, or they can simply watch others and be rewarded vicariously by observing their behaviours being rewarded. These concepts of modelling, imitation, observational learning and vicarious learning are valuable considerations for the customer service trainer and in the field of Human Resource Development:

> Behaviour modelling techniques, based on Social Learning Theory, can be used to help learners form mental models of appropriate behaviour. This technique involves presenting the skill to be learned, viewing an appropriate model or example of how the behaviour is accomplished, discussing the effectiveness of the behaviour, practicing the behaviour, and providing corrective feedback. To achieve the most training benefits, behaviour modelling techniques should incorporate practice, simulations, and role-plays (Gibson, 2004, p. 204).

If appropriate service behaviours are well established and maintained by intermittent reinforcement they will be very stable, even in the absence of any direct supervision.

Cautionary notes

While Skinner (1953) and Bandura (1969, 1986) are early theorists in the field of behaviour and motivation, many of the concepts remain relevant and have been utilized as elements in later theoretical models, some of which will be reviewed in later chapters. Steers et al. (2004) provide an outstanding historical review of motivation theories and go on to suggest that these theories need to be adapted for the contemporary workplace. Stajkovic and Luthans (2003, p. 184) in their meta-analysis of behavioural management in organizations suggest that:

> in addition to providing reinforcers, what is needed for performance improvement is further improvement of employees' competencies through training programs that increase the knowledge of the task, improve skill levels, and help to develop better task strategies.

These authors also caution against attempting to achieve unrealistic performance levels which can lead to failure and stress:

> thus a managerial challenge here is to distinguish between reinforcing qualified people versus inflating the competence perceptions (by attractive reinforcers) of unqualified employees.

Their study also looked at three extrinsic reinforcers, money, feedback and social recognition. In their meta-analysis, they determined that money improved performance 23%, social recognition 17% and feedback 10%.

> Although managers have intuitively known the importance of providing social recognition for desirable behaviours, our meta-analysis provides evidence that social recognition does indeed have a significant impact on social performance (Stajkovic and Luthans, 2003, p. 178).

Where all three reinforcers were combined as an intervention, performance improved 45%, supporting theorizing that each reinforcer covers a different aspect of the motivational domain. These authors point out that in behavioural management research, most studies have used low complexity tasks and suggest that feedback on performance may have a more important role to play in complex tasks. Of particular interest is the research that has shown how extrinsic reinforcement can undermine intrinsic motivation. For this reason, extrinsic rewards should be used initially to establish learning and only when the learner is not intrinsically motivated by interest.

Summary

This chapter has dealt with what is arguably the most important principle of training effectiveness: the trainee needs the opportunity to observe effective practice and imitate it so that he or she can receive appropriate feedback and reinforcement. Modelling can be used to shape the development of professional customer service competence. Briefing and debriefing can be used to highlight communication decisions and reinforce learning. Most challenging of all for trainers is the ability to articulate what good customer service looks and sounds like since it is often unique to the context. Verbal coding of desired behavioural outcomes can contribute dramatically to the effectiveness of observational learning and the trainer's role is to facilitate this process. Finally, feedback and social reinforcement play an important role in motivation.

On reflection

In the case study that follows, you will immediately realize that the primary relationship for the franchise operator is with the dog owner and not the barking dog. Customer service and modification of the customer's behaviour is paramount!

Beat the Barker, Home Dog Training Franchise
(the choice of name is not ideal)

As a Beat the Barker franchise operator you will enjoy interesting and rewarding work, dealing with dogs and their owners, all of whom are quite unique. The solutions provided by our behaviour modification techniques have outstanding success. Customer satisfaction survey results and testimonials are included in the attached portfolio. As you can see, as a behavioural therapist, you will enjoy many successes. Our techniques work, our customers are delighted. Even neighbours contact us to thank us!

Advantages to the franchisee

Beat the Barker is well-established with over 200 operators in this country alone; our system is positive; most of our customers come to us through word of mouth referrals; and we have used our methods successfully in over 20 countries. This type of business is flexible, enabling you to decide on the number of customers you can deal with and when you are available.

As the trainer of the new franchise operators (dog trainers) answer the following questions:

1 Describe the customer service provided by this type of franchise.

2 Anyone who agrees to run a franchise dog training business needs to be trained as part of the franchisee agreement. How would you go about training the new franchisee as a dog therapist?

3 What are the risks if the franchise operator (dog therapist) does not follow the formula or reach the required customer service performance standard?

4 How would you, as the franchisor of Beat the Barker, monitor the customer service performance standards of therapists and ensure that the training you have provided is carried out on the job in a sustainable way?

References

Bandura, A. (1969) *Principles of Behaviour Modification.* Holt, Rinehart and Winston, New York.

Bandura, A. (1986) *Social foundations of thought and action: a social cognitive theory.* Prentice Hall, Englewood Cliffs.

Bandura, A. and Mischel, W. (1965) The influence of models in modifying delay gratification patterns. *Journal of Personality and Social Psychology,* **2,** 698–705.

Boni, N. and Wilson, C. (1994) *Improving customer service in the police station through organisational behaviour management.* National Police Research Unit, Payneham.

Domjan, M. (2003) *The principles of learning and behaviour,* 5th edn. Wadsworth/Thomson Learning, Belmont.

Gibson, S. (2004) Social learning (cognitive) theory and implications for human resource development. *Advances in Developing Human Resources,* **6**(2), 193–210.

Skinner, B.F. (1953) *Science and human behaviour.* Macmillan, New York.

Stajkovic, A. and Luthans, F. (2003) Behavioural management and task performance in organizations. *Personnel Psychology,* **56,** 155–186.

Steers, M., Mowday, R. and Shapiro, D. (2004) The future of work motivation theory. *Academy of Management Review,* **29**(3), 379–387.

5

Leadership and Motivation

Another problem that may arise is that the training is inappropriate. That is, training may concentrate on areas which increase productivity or efficiency, but not customer service. Furthermore, the customer service programmes may emphasize areas which customers do not consider important. For instance, the programmes may be training services providers on how to smile, how to respond to a certain situation, rather than providing service providers with skills to enable them to foresee customer needs and wants and to be able to respond in a very personal and customized manner to that customer's needs or wants.

McColl-Kennedy and White, 1997, p. 36

Central theme

Qualities of effective leadership have implications for effective service provision. Contingency theory suggests that there are many variables that can affect the customer's level of satisfaction and the service provider needs to be responsive to all situational contingencies.

Training implications

1 By highlighting the most widely accepted dimensions of service, the *procedural* (task) and *personal* (people), the learner can be introduced to the idea that appropriate customer service might differ from one situation to the next.

2 As a trainer attentive to these two dimensions, one would ensure that training does not focus on only one dimension, for example procedure (e.g. how to process payment) without acknowledgement of the personal dimension (e.g. talking to the customer and saying farewell).

3 The learner needs to perform tasks and interact with the customer concurrently. He or she needs to be both efficient and convivial.

4 Situational variables can be analysed further in terms of *customer differences* such as demographic (e.g. age), stage in decision process, time available, mood etc.

5 Other situational variables could be analysed in terms of the *working environment* such as safety, policies, queue management etc.

6 Variables in the wider *business environment* could include legal compliance, customer rights, competitor service provision.

7 The level of complexity of scenarios or role plays analysed in training can differ according to the variables developed above.

8 Expectancy theory reminds us that the learner needs to perceive that the performance level demanded is achievable and the outcome positive. The risk is that the trainee may be overwhelmed by all potential situational variables. The level of complexity needs to be managed carefully by the trainer.

Introduction

This chapter will continue to build on emerging theoretical perspectives in organizational behaviour. In particular, the historical development of leadership theory has much to offer to enlighten trainers in the field of customer service in the parallels and insights it offers.

Research in the 1940s and early 1950s (Stogdill and Coons, 1951) focused on the characteristics or traits of effective leaders in much the same way as Chapter Three of this book focused on the emotional intelligence or social capability that the employee brings to the customer service situation.

However, this search for leadership traits was abandoned as there was little consistency in the findings. It was found, for example, that a charismatic leader may be effective in one situation, but not in another. This led Stogdill and Coons (1951) to conclude that a person does not become a leader by virtue of the possession of specific individual traits or some combination of traits. Rather, leadership is context based. Similarly, one cannot isolate one or more traits to identify the ideal customer service employee. This is certainly supported by findings that show that there were no significant differences between service-oriented employees and non-service-oriented employees on traits such as introversion or enthusiasm (Domm, 1968). In contrast, Hurley (1998) attests that effective service providers in fast food stores tend to be higher on extroversion and agreeableness.

Despite these contradictory findings, it may be that, like leadership, there is no single definition of what traits comprise a good customer service style that suits every situation. Both are complex and situationally bound.

Two-dimensional theories

In the 1970s, the trend was to look closely at leadership behaviours. Emerging theories looked at two-dimensional models such as the managerial grid (Blake and Mouton, 1978) in which one dimension was 'concern for people' and the other 'concern for production'. It was assumed that the best leader had equally high concern for both task and people, which led writers to label this a 'best way' theory, indicating that an equal concern for both people and task was essential.

In the field of customer relations, Martin (1989, 2001) suggests that service has two dimensions, personal and procedural, and these dimensions are illustrated in Table 5.1. As can be seen, these dimensions closely resemble those of the behavioural leadership theorists of the time (Lewin and Lippitt, 1938; Blake and Mouton, 1978).

According to Martin (2001), the personal dimension of service is enhanced by emphasizing positive attitude through appearance, body language, voice qualities and telephone manner. This attitude is further communicated by staying energized. This word 'energized' is a most useful one for trainers to use when describing a style of service. In Australia (the author's home), service is often described as 'laid back' which is supposed to be a compliment!

To illustrate this model, we can use the example of a fine dining experience in an expensive silver service restaurant. New employees in training for a fine dining restaurant are taught to serve vegetables with a fork and spoon. During

Table 5.1 Procedural and personal dimensions of service

Procedural dimension of service (procedures and how things get done)	Personal dimension of service (the human side of service)
Timing of service encounter	Appearance and personal presentation
Flow of service delivery system	Attitude expressed through body language and tone of voice
Accommodation and flexibility in meeting customer expectations	Attentiveness, recognizing individuality
Anticipation of customer's needs	Tact and choice of words
Communication in the service delivery system	Guidance in decision-making
Customer feedback systems and analysis	Selling skills
Organization and supervision	Gracious problem-solving

Adapted from Martin, W. (1989) *Managing quality customer service*, Crisp Publications, Los Antos, California.

this training, they normally use raw potatoes and onions to simulate the real situation, and are only let loose on the cooked vegetables once they have some experience. A trainer who feels comfortable that a waiter can demonstrate these skills and procedures, and is therefore competent at silver service, would be grossly negligent. Training, in this context, also requires the presence of the customer. The customer has high expectations of an expensive, top of the range restaurant. Attentiveness, knowledgeable assistance with menu selection, perfect timing of courses, conversation (as required, cues are provided by those around the table) and discrete clearing of courses are just a few of the personal dimensions of service in this context. This example supports the Martin (1989) model in which attention is paid to both personal and procedural dimensions in quality service situations, as shown in Figure 5.1.

Thus, it is a useful model for trainers to consider. However, one must also give some thought to other service contexts, in this case, for example, to the fast food outlet. Here, procedures have priority in order to achieve accurate scheduling and speedy service. Limited time is available for customer interaction; the personal dimension is limited and often scripted. Martin (2001) calls this 'factory style' service, high on procedure and low on personal dimensions. The question is whether there are situations in which the customer actively seeks a factory style experience, for example buying drive-through hamburgers and fries on the way to a football match. In leadership theory, the parallel to this is an environment in which concern for production could be dominant (Lewin and Lippitt, 1938).

The contribution that this theoretical perspective provides is the emphasis it places on the personal dimensions of service which are sometimes neglected by trainers. Hospital patients complain that nurses are efficient but lack a good bedside manner. This is the personal dimension of the service they expect. In all service situations, ranging from retail to real estate, customers expect personal attention as well as technical information and assistance.

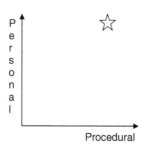

Figure 5.1 Personal and procedural dimensions of service

Situational theories of leadership

Situational theories of leadership suggest that the leader must pay attention to a number of contingencies and respond appropriately in each situation. Different situations require different styles of leadership. One well known situational leadership model is that of Hersey and Blanchard (1977) in which the authors argue that leadership style needs to change to match the (job) maturity level of followers. If we follow this model into the realm of customer service, we might conclude that the regular customer expects different treatment to the new customer and that, indeed, all customers are at different stages in their relationship with the organization. This would allow us to modify the Hersey and Blanchard (1977) model to create a 'customer maturity model' in which the novice customer needs a *telling style* to assist with product and procedure orientation, followed by a *selling style* in which the relationship moves into selling mode. Following this, the customer is conversant with products and procedures but still requires *supportive* behaviour from the salesperson. Finally, the loyal and long-term customer is largely independent, wishing to save time and make his or her own decisions, the customer is thus *delegated* the role of direction and support (Figure 5.2).

There are numerous studies that identify the many situational variables that the leader needs to consider. In this example, we have introduced the variable of customer maturity. Other variables could include the level of complexity of the decision or the authority that the customer carries for making a final purchase

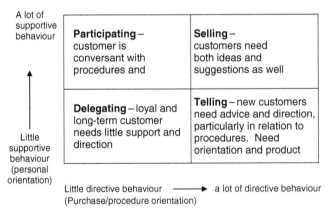

Figure 5.2 Customer maturity model (Adapted from Hersey and Blanchard, 1977)

decision, 'I might talk to my wife about that'. Customer service is also situated in a specific context of time, space, culture and organization. Fashion is quite often the driving force for consumer decision-making and being an arbiter of fashion is yet another complex challenge faced by sales people who are asked, 'Is this too old for me? Do I look good in this?'. Other variables include the time of day, number of other customers waiting and the level of assistance provided with decision-making. Large superstores, for example, do not provide staff to offer advice, even on high ticket price items such as computers and televisions.

Contingency approaches

The Martin (1989, 2001) model for quality customer service emphasizes two dimensions of service, procedural and personal. Technical skills and knowledge should be taught in conjunction with interpersonal communication with the customer. The hairdresser needs to cut and converse simultaneously, the nurse needs to inject and empathize, and the mechanic needs to listen attentively to fulsome explanations of the car's idiosyncrasies.

Contingency theories of leadership remind us that customer service is complex and multifaceted. What works with one customer will not work with another. Different approaches are required at different times to suit different needs. Customers vary depending on some of the following factors:

- time available (trainers might like to simulate the dawdling customer and the one in a hurry)

- mood (trainers might like to simulate changes in mood and consequent changes in response from the service provider)

- stage in the decision-making process (is this a pre-purchase decision, a post-purchase warranty issue?)

- perception of cost and value (the importance of the decision will vary the customer's expectations, wedding products and arrangements being the most challenging of customer service situations!).

For the classroom trainer, the challenge is to identify these situational variables and to use them to vary the scenarios or case studies provided. This idea will be discussed in more detail in a later chapter. What this does tell us is that customer service principles cannot be taught as simple step-by-step processes without a variety of situational variables to complicate decision-making and highlight the range of possibilities that emerge in each unique interaction with the customer. For example, an employee might say, 'I did not help the older customer as I had two people at the counter and she appeared to be happy to take her time even though she arrived first'. This is just one of many potential situational variables used in this context for decision-making.

Expectancy theory of motivation

The model of motivation, proposed by Victor Vroom (1973), explains why people choose to follow certain actions. The first is valence – how important the expected outcome of the behaviour is to the individual. The second is expectancy – how strongly the individual believes their behaviour will be linked to a successful outcome. The third is instrumentality – how confident the individual is that their behaviour will be rewarded as they desire. Specifically, such questions will be in the mind of the individual:

- Effort and performance: how hard will I have to work to achieve the level of performance?

- Performance and reward: if I achieve the performance level what reward (if any) is there?

- Reward/s: how attractive is the reward? Is it worth making the effort?

The individual may perceive that after making the effort to achieve the performance level demanded by the organization, the outcomes will be either positive, such as pay, tips, customer satisfaction etc., or negative, such as boredom, fatigue and pressure from colleagues to wind back productivity. The last of these is a common response when others in the group feel that one member is setting the performance standard too high, 'if you clean 14 hotel rooms, they will expect us all to do the same'.

Effort $\Rightarrow$ performance $\Rightarrow$ rewards $\Rightarrow$ attractiveness of rewards

Figure 5.3 Simplified model of expectancy theory

This theory links some previous discussions about the antecedents and consequences of behaviour. It also introduces the idea that different workers have different perceptions about their capabilities and the outcomes that they favour. Mann (2006), however, argues that this theory has limited applicability in the public service sector where many employees are motivated to have an impact on community affairs and have a deep desire to make a difference. Mann suggests that expectancy theory is a rational choice theory with an emphasis on extrinsic rewards. She reaches the conclusion that:

> the most important lesson from these competing and complementary theories is that none of them will suffice for all occasions for all employees; management should instead follow a contingency approach, drawing upon knowledge of the various theories to address different individuals in different situations (Mann, 2006, p. 36).

In practice

In a discussion with two other people, describe a specific part of your work experience in customer service in terms of your perceptions of the effort required to reach the sales targets; your capacity to reach and sustain performance at that level; the incentives offered; and the value that you placed on these rewards.

The trainer as leader

A trainer is a leader and a motivator. In terms of establishing goals for learning, close attention needs to be paid to the perceptions of the trainee with regard to the level of effort and difficulty, as well as the value of the outcomes of training. Equally important is the expectancy of success as a function of particular contexts. Organizational factors, such as insufficient staff, software problems, systems failures and the like, may emerge when training begins and employees say, 'this won't work' and 'it's not worth it'. Their expectancy of success would be appropriately low with the consequent lowering of their motivation. Indeed, Rutherford Silvers (2005), looking at goal orientation, finds that studies examining goal orientation's relationship with salesperson performance produce inconsistent results and therefore postulates that, for some employees, performance-avoidance goal orientation is grounded in fear of failure.

Goal orientation

Theorists Locke and Latham (2002) are well known for their extensive research into motivation, specifically the relationship between goal setting and task performance. One of the factors they have explored in depth is the relationship of goal difficulty to performance, with studies showing that the most difficult goals produce the highest levels of effort and performance. A second feature of effective goal setting is specificity – in other words, specific goals reduce ambiguity and improve performance. These authors suggest the following:

- goals serve a directive function in that they direct effort toward goal-relevant activities

- goals have an energizing function, with high goals leading to greater effort than low goals

- goals affect persistence

- goals affect action (people use task-relevant knowledge and strategies).

As Figure 5.4 illustrates, there are several moderators of goal setting, the first being goal commitment by the individual. Secondly, goal commitment is linked to goal importance which can be enhanced through visionary leadership and support. Self-efficacy is the third moderator: leaders (and trainers) can enhance self-efficacy by developing increased mastery through success experiences. Feedback is another important moderator, providing the individual with information needed to evaluate progress towards a goal. Finally, assuming that people have the requisite skills, goals that are moderately difficult (task complexity) seem to have the best effects on motivation and self-regulated performance. Goal difficulty does not bear a linear relationship to performance. Overly easy goals do not motivate; neither are people motivated to attempt what they believe are impossible goals.

Goal setting and attainment enhance self-regulation through their effects on motivation, learning, self-efficacy (perceived capabilities for learning or performing actions at given levels) and self-evaluations of progress. Goals motivate

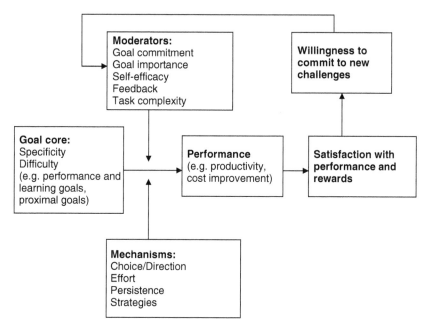

Figure 5.4 Essential elements of goal-setting theory and the high-performance cycle (Locke and Latham, 2002, p. 714)

people to exert effort necessary to meet task demands and persist over time. Goals also direct individuals' attention to relevant task features, behaviours to be performed, and potential outcomes, and goals can affect how people process information. Goals help people focus on the task, select and apply appropriate strategies and monitor goal progress. Goal attainment builds self-efficacy and leads people to select new, challenging goals.

Summary

Customer service has at least two dimensions, procedure (task) and people (relationship). Both dimensions need to be considered and accommodated. In training, the customer should always be 'present'. If the real customer is not there, then a case study, simulation, game or role play is needed to develop the trainee's communication expertise in parallel with their technical expertise. Customer service is situated in a complex environment and the decision factors that the service employee uses to choose a course of action need to be highlighted. The trainee must perceive that the service standard set by the organization is achievable and valuable on a personal level. Building self-efficacy through goal setting develops confidence and encourages people to set their own goals and to self-evaluate their progress towards goal attainment.

CASE STUDY

Associated Airlines Inc

Our vision is to make air travel a positive experience for every customer at every stage of their journey. We aim to provide the most professional standards in safety and systems to ensure that the experience is trouble free. Further than that, we aim to provide the friendliest experience of any airline. Our company values its people, those on the ground and in the air and this is reflected in the exemplary service standards demonstrated towards you, our valuable customers.

As with most other airlines, employees need to be familiar with a wide range of policies which help to answer questions from customers and resolve emerging issues such as delayed or cancelled flights. Clearly, in this situation, there are two components to the training, procedural and personal. Employees need to understand the correct ticketing and refund procedures and, at the same time, need to build the relationship with the customer.

Questions

1 Policies and procedures are summarized in the following table. Elaborate on the approach you would take to developing communication skills for a call centre position with an airline (including verbal communication attributes such as vocabulary, articulation, volume and other voice qualities).

2 In planning the sequence of training, describe whether you would develop knowledge relating to policies first and communications second, or develop both simultaneously. Justify your position.

3 Write a training plan, including learning objectives for the first three hour training session with airline call centre staff.

4 Discuss the possible perceptions that trainees might have that this is 'too hard' and explain how you would ensure that trainees felt that the training objectives are achievable and desirable.

5 Explain how you might use the concept of contingency responsiveness in training.

Reservations	Accompanied travel for children
Ticketing	Travel assistance for seniors
Check-in	Delays and cancellations
Denied boarding	On board service
Baggage handling	On board meals
Baggage allowances and excesses	Medical emergencies
Oversized baggage	Missed connections
Lost baggage	Refunds

References

Blake, R.R. and Mouton, J.S. (1978) *The new managerial grid: strategic new insights into a proven system for increasing organization productivity and individual effectiveness, plus a revealing examinatin of how your managerial style can affect your mental and physical health*, 2nd edn. Gulf Pub. Co. Book Division, Houston.

Domm, D.R. (1968) A study of personality, attitude toward others, and attitude toward service of the service-oriented employee. Ohio State University, Michigan.

Hersey, P. and Blanchard, K.H. (1977) *Management of organizational behavior: utilizing human resources*, 3rd edn. Prentice Hall, Englewood Cliffs.

Hurley, R. (1998) Customer service behaviour in retail settings: a study of the effect of service provider personality. *Journal of the Academy of Marketing Science*, **26**(2), 115–127.

Lewin, K. and Lippitt, R. (1938) An experimental approach to the study of autocracy and democracy. *Sociometry*, **1**, 292–300.

Locke, E. and Latham, G. (2002) Building a practically useful theory of goal setting and task motivation. *American Psychologist*, **57**(9), 705–717.

Mann, G. (2006) A motive to serve. *Public Personnel Management*, **35**(1), 33–41.

Martin, W. (1989) *Managing quality customer service*. Crisp Publications, Los Antos.

Martin, W. (2001) *Quality customer service*, 3rd edn. Crisp Publications, New York.

McColl-Kennedy, A. and White, T. (1997) Service provider training programs at odds with customer requirements in five star hotels. *Journal of Services Marketing*, **11**(4), 249–264.

Rutherford Silvers, J. (2005) *Standards: fear or the future?* Mark Sonder Productions, viewed 12 December 2005 <http://marksonderproductions.com/about/News/Feb05Standards.html>

Stogdill, R. and Coons, A. (eds) (1951) *Leader behaviour: its description and measurement*. Research Monograph No. 88, Ohio State University.

Vroom, V. (1973) *Work and motivation*. John Wiley and Sons, New York.

6

Competency-Based
Training

Sitting at the core of all services industries businesses is the provision of good customer service. The customer bases for these industries are increasingly sophisticated and have rapidly rising expectations of value. Survival and growth within these industries is driven by meeting and exceeding these expectations. In a people intensive industry, meeting consumer and customer service demand is the paramount driver of skill needs.

ANTA, 2005, p. 3

Central theme

The competency movement aims to develop holistic descriptors of workplace performance. The benefits of this system are that performance can be exhibited both on and off the job, making training portable within educational systems and between college and workplace. Primarily, competency approaches work towards improvements in vocational training.

Training implications

1 Since competency-based training is expressed in terms of outcomes, the trainer needs to decide whether the learner can use their existing knowledge and workplace experience to demonstrate attainment using *recognition of prior learning* (RPL) or *recognition of current competence* (RCC).

2 Workplace-based candidates may be able to use *learning contracts* to negotiate ways in which they can achieve the performance as part of their daily work, thus contributing directly to personal and organizational goals.

3 Novice candidates entering a competency-based system may need a carefully structured learning program covering underpinning knowledge, basic skills and a range of workplace practices.

4 The workplace environment can become more realistic to college students with case studies, role plays, scenario analysis, problem-solving and simulation as part of training and assessment design.

5 The more holistic the final assessment, the more representative of the workplace environment it is likely to be. Breaking down competencies into atomistic behaviours is generally counterproductive.

Introduction

Many countries, including many in the European Union, as well as Australia, New Zealand and South Africa, have introduced systems of competency-based training. Primarily, the purpose of this is to ensure that vocational training in all sectors reflects the needs of industry. In addition to this, a secondary aim is that training should be nationally consistent whether conducted on or off the job, giving individuals the opportunity to participate in lifelong, widely recognized training. In some cases, organizations have gone further to customize nationally devised competency units to meet the specific needs of their business enterprises. Others have gone further still, devising for themselves a unique range of competency units, such as Qantas Airways in Australia.

What is competency-based training?

Competency-based training purports to improve vocational and workplace training. Essentially, industry bodies provide descriptors of training outcomes which then form the basis for widely recognized, consistent and portable qualifications. Broadly speaking, a competency is the ability to perform activities within an occupation to the standard expected in employment.

A competency unit (such as one for Customer Service) includes:

■ elements of competency

■ performance criteria

■ a range of variables statement.

Elements of competency are the basic building blocks of a unit of competency. They describe, in outcome terms, functions a person is able to perform in a particular area of work. The elements combine to make up the unit. Performance criteria are evaluative statements specifying what is to be assessed and the required level of performance. The range of variables statement indicates the scope of application of the competency. A range statement links the required knowledge and organizational and technical requirements to a context. It describes any contextual variables that will be used or encountered when applying the competency in a workplace situation. An example from the UK Customer Service NVQ Level 3 is illustrated in Table 6.1. While this is only a small part of a competency unit, a complete unit is included in Appendix A.

Table 6.1 NVQ Level 3 Customer Service

Unit 3 Develop Positive Working Relationships with Customers	
Element 3.2	Present positive personal image to customer
Performance criteria	3.2.1 Treatment of customers is always courteous and helpful even when under stress
	3.2.2 Standards for appearance and behaviour are consistently maintained
	3.2.3 Equipment and supplies used in transactions with customers are available, up to date and in good order
	3.2.4 Customers are advised of appropriate statutory measures operation to protect their health and safety
	3.2.5 Opportunities for improving working relationships with customers are actively sought
Range to which the element applies	Equipment and supplies: ■ Literature ■ Stationery/forms ■ Small stores ■ Consumables ■ Mechanical/electronic consumable Communication: ■ Face to face ■ Written ■ Telephonic

Source: RSA Examinations Board, Coventry

Debates have raged for the past two decades over this approach to workplace training. In summary the protagonists argue that:

■ The units of competency assist with the description of a field of work, occupation or profession

■ The units of competency, when adopted across the whole system, on and off the job, allow portability of qualifications for individuals moving from one college to another, from one job to another or from one qualification to another. They take the units with them as a form of training currency, sometimes even from one country to another

- Candidates can seek recognition of prior learning against the competency unit, based on their evidence of life and work experience.

Those who argue against a competency-based system say that:

- The units, elements and variables often become atomistic to the point that they are valueless

- There is a tendency to focus on easily described observable skills at the expense of complex workplace decision-making

- The competency units are unsuitable as a form of curriculum. Reid and Johnson (1999) define the curriculum as those discursive practices which affect what and how students learn, and what and how teachers teach. Teaching is a scaffolding process and curriculum should assist with the teaching process and not simply describe occupational outcomes

- Students/learners emerge from the system without a grounding in knowledge or theory

- Competency-based training neglects general educational achievement such as literacy and numeracy.

Part of the problem with the competency approach is developing a common understanding of what competence means. A study by Weinhart (2001) reveals that there is no single use of the concept of competence and no broadly accepted definition or unifying theory.

Model for competence

The Organisation for Economic Co-operation and Development has undertaken extensive research in this area, with a particular focus on key competencies for a successful life and a well-functioning society (Rychen and Sagalnik, 2001). Their project, DeSeCo (Definition and Selection of Competencies) has produced a holistic model to illustrate the concept of competence and this is illustrated in Figure 6.1. This conceptualization of competence 'combines components that together represent the complex control system and results in a person taking action' (Rychen and Sagalnik, 2001, p. 44). Thus, in the illustration, the ability to cooperate requires the mobilization of internal structures such as knowledge,

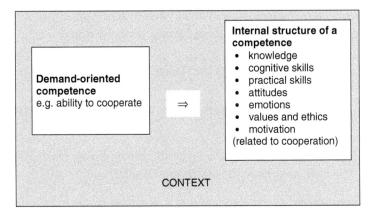

Figure 6.1 The demand defines the internal structure of a competence (Source: Rychen and Sagalnik (2002) *Defining and selection of competencies: theoretical and conceptual foundations (DeSeCo)* p. 44)

cognitive skills, emotions and motivation. As the authors point out, possessing a competence means that one can select, mobilize and orchestrate resources, at an appropriate time and in a complex situation.

One of the features of this model is its emphasis on the context dependency of competence. As Rychen and Sagalnik point out, 'actions always take place in a social or socio-cultural environment, in a context that is structured into multiple social fields' (Rychen and Sagalnik, 2001, p. 46). The topic of context will be a recurring one in the chapters that follow.

Generic competencies

Discussion on the subject of generic skills for vocational education and training has been widespread and implementation has been through several phases in recent years. Known also as key competencies, core skills, key skills and basic skills, all refer to similar common elements. Key skills usually include communication skills that contribute to productive and harmonious relations between employees and customers. Key competencies from the DeSeCo project are summarized in Table 6.2.

The DeSeCo project is likely to have a wide impact as it is supported by the OECD and incorporates contributions from major disciplines such as sociology and economics. In these reports, the generic competencies identified (Rychen

Table 6.2   Key competencies from the DeSeCo project

Competency Category 1: Using tools interactively

A. Use language, symbols and texts interactively

B. Use knowledge and information interactively

C. Use technology interactively

Competency Category 2: Interacting in heterogeneous groups

A. Relate well to others

B. Cooperate, work in teams

C. Manage and resolve conflicts

Competency Category 3: Acting autonomously

A. Act within the big picture

B. Form and conduct life plans and personal projects

C. Defend and assert rights, interests, limits and needs

---

and Sagalnik, 2001) allow comparisons between countries. However, as Hager (2005) explains, 'as best available theoretical accounts of learning at work suggest, the contextuality of actual work processes severely curtails naïve expectations of unproblematic generic transfer' (p. 4). Nonetheless, the model developed for this project clarifies the concept of context. Context is shown in the theoretical and conceptual foundation of the DeSeCo work (Rychen and Sagalnik, 2001) as both the immediate surroundings and the larger socio-economic and political environment.

Contexts for service competence

Service industries are numerous, could include those listed in Table 6.3 and potentially many more. Each provides a different context, different types of customer, at different stages of the decision-making process.

As one can tell from the above list, the services industry as defined in Australia covers a wide scope. Consequently, the debate over the generic nature of competence in the delivery of quality customer service becomes extremely important. Each of the listed industries provides a vastly different context for service, a topic which will be re-visited in a later chapter that discusses the concept that learning is 'situated' and inseparable from context.

Table 6.3 Service Industries Australia

Caravan industry	Retail industry
Community pharmacy industry	Wholesale industry
Floristry industry	Tourism industry
Funeral services industry	Events industry
Hospitality industry	Sport industry
Beauty industry	Outdoor recreation and fitness industry
Community recreation industry	Hairdressing industry

Source: ANTA 2005, *Industry Skills Report, Services Industry Skills Council*, Department of Education, Science and Training, Canberra

Any training solution offered to meet the emerging needs for customer service training across these diverse industries, economies and cultures needs to be carefully considered. A 'have a nice day' approach is not suitable for all workplace contexts, particularly those where customers are seeking an experience that is culturally authentic and quite unique. Marketing gurus would be aghast at the possibility of uniformity when the catchcry is differentiation from competitors, 'Our unique service is our point of difference'.

In practice

Questions

1 Use three adjectives to describe your customer service experiences or expectations with any or all of the following:

- Checkout operator
- Registrar of births, deaths and marriages
- Recruitment agent
- Car sales person
- Business advisor
- Call centre
- Private detective.

For example, you might hope that the service provided by the last is 'discrete'.

2 Discuss the implications of these differences for training.

Organizational development

In a sophisticated analysis of the human resource practices that support the development of customer-oriented behaviour, Peccei and Rosenthal (2001) tested three models using data from a large-scale survey covering 2100 staff in seven retail stores. The interventions included in the program included supportive leadership, management role modelling, job redesign and customer care training, all of which were aimed at producing a sense of psychological empowerment among employees. The results show that this in turn enhanced customer-oriented behaviour and led the researchers to conclude that there is unambiguous support for the full mediation model of customer-oriented behaviour.

> Specifically, two main findings emerged from the study. The first is the positive association between all three dimensions of psychological empowerment and customer orientation. Autonomy, internalization of service values and a sense of competence were all related to customer-orientation, with internalization emerging as the strongest drive of customer oriented behaviours. The second is that all the perceived management behaviours and HR practices examined were linked to customer oriented behaviours but only indirectly, through their impact on empowerment. Supervisors who were perceived to be supportive and customer oriented contributed to all three dimensions of employee empowerment, while perceived role modelling and supportive leadership by management contributed to the internalization and autonomy dimensions of empowerment, but had no significant impact on employees' felt job competence (Peccei and Rosenthal, 2001, p. 851).

Thus, as Figure 6.2 illustrates, job competence is only one part of a human resource management strategy.

This important study highlights some of the considerations and perspectives that need further investigation, including the following questions:

- how is the service vision developed and communicated in the organization?

- how is a service culture sustained?

- how does training contribute to customer service excellence?

- can training alone contribute or are other human resources practices important?

- how important is role modelling, leadership and empowerment?

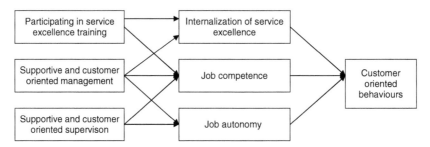

Figure 6.2 Full mediation model for developing customer oriented behaviours. (Source: Peccei and Rosenthal, 2001, p. 838)

This will lead on to further discussion on the specifics of customer service training, design, delivery and evaluation:

- what type of adult learning needs to occur (on and off the job) in relation to customer service?

- can the outcomes of such learning be best expressed in behavioural terms (competence)?

- is customer service a generic skill or is it situation specific?

- how can optimal skills transfer occur from off job training to the workplace context?

- how can skills transfer be facilitated from college to workplace, one job context to another, indeed from one service incident to another?

- is there a more sophisticated cognitive process occurring in the development of expertise in this area?

- how do the job contexts for customer service vary and what are some of the key decision factors used by service personnel in dealing with different situations?

- how can we evaluate the success of training?

Workplace training

When a group of trainers get together, their debate about the nature of competence can be heated and paralysing. When stakeholders cannot agree on definitions, they often cannot progress with the concept. Yet many organizations have

Table 6.4 Competency unit: Manage quality service

Unit: Manage Quality Customer Service	
Element 3 Monitor, adjust and review customer service	
Performance criteria	3.1 Strategies to monitor progress in achieving product and/or service targets and standards are developed and used
	3.2 Strategies to obtain customer feedback are developed and used to improve the provision of products and/or services
	3.3 Resources are developed, procured and used effectively to provide quality products and/or services to customers
	3.4 Decisions to overcome problems and to adapt customer service and products and/or service delivery are taken in consultation with appropriate individuals and groups
	3.5 Records, reports and recommendations are managed within the organization's systems and processes

Source: NTIS

successfully used this approach as the basis for training and development and for performance assessment across the organization. Where this is the case, its value as a human resource management tool is judged by the stakeholders, such as senior management, employees and the unions. Competency standards can help to define career paths and they can provide a sound basis for workplace learning which emphasizes outcomes achieved in the real context of the job environment. Take for example part of the competency unit for managing customer service used in Australia illustrated in Table 6.4 (NTIS, 2004).

Using this competency unit a manager responsible for service in a super-market could apply the unit and develop the strategies, resources and records suggested. The aim of the learning exercise would be personally relevant and organizationally productive. The same unit could be used by a manager super-vising service in a call centre. Herein lies the greatest benefit of this approach for workplace learning.

Learning contracts

For employees who are based in workplaces, a most valuable training tool is a negotiated learning contract. This is made possible with the development of competency standards that define outcomes that can be achieved in the place of work. In this situation, the assessor collaborates with the candidate to develop a plan of action for assembling evidence that the learning outcomes have been achieved. Instructions on how to develop and negotiate learning contracts are included in Appendix B. As an alternative to this, a broad, open-ended assessment, such as the one that follows, can be used to enable the candidate to demonstrate competence on the job. In this case, the task is assigned to a manager and the outcomes relate to building quality service systems.

In practice

The following competency based assessment has wide application and the potential for meaningful outcomes.

Part one

In the last assessment you identified one area in which a service improvement could occur. You analysed some data which gave you the basis for this potential service improvement. In this assessment you will continue this process by working through the following steps:

- Develop a goal for service improvement

- Develop specific objectives or targets for service improvement

- Analyse internal and external factors

- Establish priorities

- Set timelines

- Consult with colleagues

- Look at resource implications

- Inform stakeholders.

You will then:

- Plan, analyse and organize the work

- Implement and monitor the plan

- Conduct and evaluate outcomes

Note: It is important that the objectives of the operational plan are *realistic and achievable* within the short space of time available for this assessment. A report using the above headings (all bullet points) is recommended.

Part two

Finally, and most importantly, you will reflect on your learning by answering the following questions:

- What did I learn?

- What will I do next time?

- How do I feel about it?

- How do other people feel about it?

- What do I need to know more about?

- Which specific competencies do I need to develop?

- How will I do this?

A report using the above headings (all bullet points) is recommended.

This assessment task needs to be reviewed with your *workplace mentor* and brief written feedback included before sending it in to your assessor.

Questions

1 Discuss whether this learning contract is applicable in more than one service industry or sector.

2 Develop examples of specific objectives or targets for two contrasting service environments.

3 If you were the assessor briefing the mentor, what would you say about their role?

The assessment illustrated enables the candidate to show how improvements in customer service have been achieved. Additionally, this assessment asks the candidate to reflect on the learning process as well as the outcome. Finally, feedback from a workplace mentor (usually a senior manager) is required so that the external assessor can validate the value of the outcomes to the organization.

Competency-based training for college-based learning

The value of competency based systems as the basis for quasi curriculum in vocational training centres and colleges remains to be proven. A different curriculum approach may be needed for novices who are not placed in a realistic workplace environment. Indeed, it can be argued that developing a workplace simulation is counter-productive since the level of realism achieved is seldom satisfactory. Secondly, and more importantly, learners may have different expectations of formal training and education provided off the job. This could include developing a wide knowledge base, exposure to theory and development of cognitive and other capabilities including literacy.

Summary

The test of any competency unit, or system based on this concept, is its utilitarian value. Does the framework support and improve workplace training? Does the framework support and improve college based vocational training? Is the system widely used on and off the job? Are the participants achieving the aims, such as portability of qualifications? Models presented in this chapter highlight the internal structure of a competence (those attributes brought to the action) and the context in which the action occurs. The complexity of the context and the inseparability of action from context will be the topic of the next chapter.

On reflection

A trainer opens a session with the following outcome:

On completion of training you will be able to describe the features and benefits of the products in this range. You will be able to list and describe procedures for processing sales and you will know about the policy for refunds.

In this example, two elements are missing. The most important of these is the customer. Secondly, this trainer does not anticipate application

---

of selling skills in a workplace environment or simulation. A written test would assess the outcome as it is stated, but this is clearly unsatisfactory. Neither outcome nor assessment is valid, they do not assess workplace competence.

1 Using the following table, develop series training outcomes so that the service provider can be deemed competent in making sales and providing refunds from a specific product line.

Given the following circumstances, conditions and knowledge	The trainee will be able to demonstrate the following	The performance level will be measured by

2 Describe how you would plan training and assessment for the outcomes described.

References

ANTA (2005) *Industry skills report, services industry skills council*. Department of Education, Science and Training, Canberra.

Hager, P. (2005) Current theories of workplace learning: a critical assessment. In *International handbook of educational policy* (N. Bascia, A. Cumming, A. Datnow, K. Lieithwood and D. Livingstone, eds). Kluwer Academic Publishers, London.

NTIS (2004) *(BSBFLM507B) Manage quality customer service*, viewed 14 April 2005 <http://www.ntis.gov.au/cgi-bin/waxhtml/~ntis2/unit.wxh?page=80&inputRef=32932&sCalledFrom=std>

Peccei, R. and Rosenthal, P. (2001) Delivering customer-oriented behaviour through empowerment: an empirical test of HRM assumptions. *Journal of Management Studies*, **38**(6), 831–857.

Reid, A. and Johnson, B. (1999) *Contesting the curriculum*. Social Science Press, Katoomba.

Rychen, D.S. and Sagalnik, L.H. (2001) *Defining and selecting key competencies*. Hogrefe & Huber, Seattle.

Weinert, F. (2001) Concept of competence: a conceptual clarification. In *Defining and selecting key competencies* (D. Rychen and L. Salganik, eds), pp. 17–31. Hogrefe & Huber, Seattle.

7

Developing Expertise

Good teaching is normative and made up of at least three components: the logical acts of teaching (defining, demonstrating, modelling, explaining, correcting, etc.); the psychological acts of teaching (caring, motivating, encouraging, rewarding, punishing, planning, evaluating, etc.); and the moral acts of teaching (showing honesty, courage, tolerance, compassion, respect, fairness, etc.). When coupled with demonstrations of student learning, we have a start toward a definition of quality in teaching.

Highly qualified teachers, then, provide evidence that certain qualities of teaching are frequently present in the everyday experiences of their students. The teacher's competence, proficiency, ability, and talent – the many synonyms for having qualifications – are demonstrated in the logical, psychological, and moral acts of teaching, along with evidence that desirable kinds of learning are taking place.

Berliner, 2005

Central theme

The development of expertise requires the trainer to focus more carefully on the learning *process* rather than on specific learning outcomes or learning as *product*. The trainer in this situation is facilitating the learning journey during which the *learner learns to learn*. Cognitive ability in the form of facility with meanings and their interconnectedness is emphasized.

Training implications

1 The levels of the cognitive domain are remembering, understanding, applying, analysing and evaluating. These levels can provide the trainer with the development of increasingly difficult learning tasks relating to customer service provision.

2 Problem-solving is one of the most effective learning strategies for college and workplace based candidates. These problem scenarios should include requirement for technical/procedural knowledge as well as interpersonal communication.

3 Using experience and informal learning as the basis for reflection, learners can capitalize on their existing schemas (a schema is a mental structure that we use to organize and simplify our knowledge of the world around us).

4 The role of judgment and the evaluation of a range of possibilities should be emphasized, often with agreement that there is no single solution but a variety of approaches.

Introduction

This chapter will put the spotlight on expertise, the ability to do something well. An expert in customer service can undertake routine tasks in a seamless and efficient way. An expert can solve problems readily. In some cases, this means being creative to the extent that the outcome is not known during the process of finding the solution. Expertise, to be recognized, is acknowledged by others in a social context, in this case in the workplace. In contrast to previous chapters, which have highlighted the affective domain (e.g. emotional intelligence) and the behavioural outcomes of training (e.g. performance targets), this chapter will look at cognitive development, the transformation of novice to expert. Where the proponents of competency based training focus on *products* or outcomes of learning, the cognitive psychologists attend to the learning *process*, the cognitive processes and the learning experiences. In doing so they stress that expertise is derived from meaning:

> An expert is regarded as someone who has considerable facility with meanings and their interconnections. An expert derives this facility from many experiences, connecting the various meanings that the experiences offer, as well as meanings that others construct on those experiences. Expertise is being able to access and utilize the rich connections among meanings that enable an expert to perform well on routine tasks and to work out ways to solve creative and other problems (Stevenson, 2003, p. 5).

In order to illustrate the importance of judgment in the display of expertise, let us look at a workplace example. Most travel agency firms have a top 100 list, based on the sales record of each agent. It is generally acknowledged by one's peers (and superiors) that you are an expert if you find yourself at the top of the list. It means that you have been able to:

■ exhibit knowledge of an extensive range of travel destinations

■ meet a diverse range of client needs

■ initiate, follow up and close sales

- maximize revenue from every customer

- differentiate big spenders from small spenders (attending to the first and neglecting the second)

- exploit commission margins.

In addition to all the above, the travel agent would need to work quickly and efficiently with a range of reservation software systems and negotiate with providers.

John Stevenson (2003) highlights the fact that expertise is socially determined, that it is historically situated. This means that what was regarded as expert customer service in the 1920s is different to what is regarded that way today. This judgment of who is expert also differs from country to country, from occupation to occupation, and from workplace to workplace. Indeed, one of the important questions is that of transfer from one situation to another. Expert individuals have the capacity to take meaning from one context and apply it to another context in order to solve problems more readily or create ideas.

In Figure 7.1, expertise is described as being connected directly to previous experience; being contextually situated in time and place; making sense through meanings and drawing on meanings in new situations. Finally, and most

importantly, this model allows for co-constructed meanings, meanings developed with others. Briefings before service periods and debriefings after service are ways in which colleagues share meanings in relation to customer service in their department. As a group, employees should be able to say, 'In our department customer service involves ...'. The chapter that follows will look more carefully at the social context of learning and at learners involved in largely unstructured group learning.

Knowing that, knowing how, wanting to know

In education, theorists differentiate between forms of learning in terms of 'knowing that' and 'knowing how'. With many diverse approaches to learning it seems

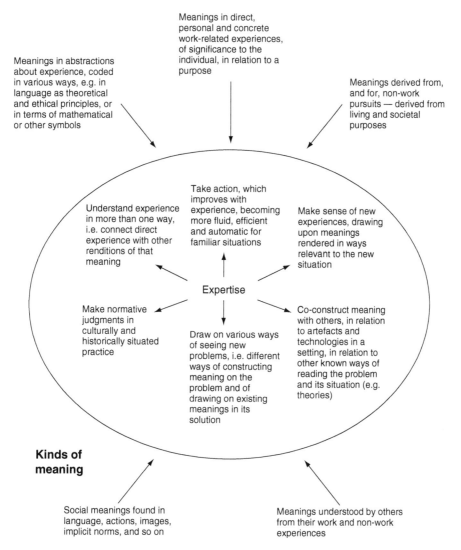

Figure 7.1 Relationships of expertise and meaning (from Stevenson, 2003, with permission)

impossible to give a scientific account of learning. Dewey (1963), a seminal figure in educational theory, stresses the importance of meaning in terms of the capacity to do and emphasizes that meaning is situated in practice. Because the environment is constantly changing, people need to adjust to new circumstances in order to live harmoniously in the environment. This involves problem-solving and reflection, important elements of the evolutionary learning process. Rogers (1983) further adds a reflection on being inspired to learn what is personally meaningful.

> I want to talk about *learning*. But *not* the lifeless, sterile, futile, quickly forgotten stuff that is crammed in to the mind of the poor helpless individual tied into his seat by ironclad bonds of conformity! I am talking about LEARNING the insatiable curiosity that drives the adolescent boy to absorb everything he can see or hear or read about gasoline engines in order to improve the efficiency and speed of his 'cruiser'. I am talking about the student who says, 'I am discovering, drawing in from the outside, and making that which is drawn in a real part of me'. I am talking about any learning in which the experience of the learner progresses along this line: 'No, no, that's not what I want'; 'Wait! This is closer to what I am interested in, what I need'; 'Ah, here it is! Now I'm grasping and comprehending what I *need* and what I want to know!'(Rogers, 1983, pp. 18–19).

For us, the environment is in the field of customer service, although this practice differs markedly across service industries such as funeral parlours, auto repair shops, hospitals, supermarkets, real estate agencies, banks, stock exchanges and telecommunications providers. Clearly, practice also differs from one workplace to another; indeed, it is the aim of the marketing department to ensure differentiation. The ambience of one restaurant could be noisy and family friendly while another is quiet and luxurious.

In practice

Our study has important implications for managers. First, it is important that all service providers, regardless of whether they are male or female, express concern for the customer; provide voice to the customer; and, when possible and reasonable, give a high level of compensation when endeavoring to recover a service failure. Our results clearly demonstrate that showing concern was critical regardless of the gender of either service provider or customer.

Second, it is important that managers recognize that male and female consumers do indeed place different values on other elements of the service recovery process. When dealing with female consumers, it is critical that female consumers be given sufficient voice during the organization's attempt at service recovery as female consumers want to be included in the service recovery. Specifically, women want their views to be heard during the recovery process and to be allowed to provide input into the recovery process. Men, in contrast, did not view voice as important.

Our study also provides further evidence for the existence of gender differences in evaluations of employee behaviour. Customers appeared to have preferences for different types of service recovery based on whether they were men or women. Indeed, it seems that female service providers rate higher on some aspects than on others, whereas male service providers rate higher on other aspects. For example, both ratings of employee effort and future intentions to return to the organization were lower when the service provider was a woman. Also, overall, male service providers were perceived as being more competent than female service providers. (McColl-Kennedy et al., 2003, p. 66)

Questions

1 Discuss the idea that there are gender differences in the way in which customers expect problems to be solved.

2 Discuss the idea that gender differences impact on both sides of the customer service interaction.

3 Debate the proposition that 'women are more expert nurses/librarians/checkout operators/call centre operators than men'. (Select your preferred role.)

Problem-solving

Middleton (2005) describes problems as 'tasks that workers encounter, and are required to solve, where there is some possible impediment to completing the task successfully' (p. 136). He uses the problem space model (Newell and Simon, 1972) to describe the way in which a person (or group) navigates from the problem state, through the problem space to the goal state. The level of difficulty in navigating through problem space is caused by:

- many elements (for example, the customer might be faced with unlimited product choices)

- contradictory needs (the purchaser may not be the decision-maker in the family and each may have different expectations)

- opaque wants (some customers don't know what they want until they find it)

- ill-defined needs (a customer purchasing the product such as a car might have little idea about his/her requirements and therefore the specifications of what is required)

- emergent criteria (the salesperson in the previous situation might find that criteria emerge over the process of the sale that are hard to satisfy)

- the need to be creative (cutting edge entertainment events are often associated with creative approaches to service).

These problem dimensions can be used by trainers to increase the complexity of customer service scenarios or case studies.

Adult learning

This theoretical framework suggests that trainers should attend to the ways in which individuals make meaning of their experiences. This is particularly important for adult learners who have a lifetime of experience as a rich resource. This can be used to support and enhance the training process. Malcolm Knowles (2005) highlights the following core principles of andragogy (adult learning theory):

- learners need to know what, why and how they will learn

- the self concept of the adult learner is autonomous and self-directing

- prior experience of the adult learner is a resource and provides mental schema

- adults have a readiness to learn which is life related

■ adults' orientation to learning is problem centred and contextual

■ adults are intrinsically motivated to learn (p. 4).

These being the case, decision-making and problem-solving are valuable approaches to take when training adults. Thus, rather than being taught about abstract principles (such as the five steps to handling a customer complaint), learners should analyse their prior customer service experiences. Problems and decisions can also be presented for analysis, being graded in terms of the level of knowledge (know what) and experience (know how) that the learners bring to the situation.

In practice

Using the travel agent as an example, problem-solving could be graduated in the following way, based on a revised taxonomy of the cognitive domain (Anderson and Krathwohl, 2001):

■ Remembering

■ Understanding

■ Applying

■ analysing

■ Evaluating.

Remembering: recognize or recall information.
    Where are the cities that the traveller wants to visit? How long will it take to travel between these cities?

Understanding: understand, organize and arrange information.
    Explain the order in which you think the traveller should visit these cities.

Applying: apply information to solve a problem.
    Plan two possible itineraries to cover all the destinations and their attractions. Put together a quote for each.

Analysing: think critically and in depth.

Explain which itinerary you would present to the customer and why. Explain ways in which you could secure the customer, upsell on travel products and close the sale. How would you deal with objections such as 'too far, too expensive, don't speak the language'. This should be done in practice, as a workplace simulation or role play. Note that the learner would need access to the itinerary, product information and prices. Ideally, a live computer system should be provided in case the customer asks for alternatives.

Also develop a new tourism product, such as a cooking tour of Italy. Provide a rationale including a competitor analysis. Cost and predict product sales. Develop a marketing campaign.

Evaluating: judge the merit of an idea, a solution to a problem.

Present your product in a sales presentation to travel retailers (or simulated). As a group, evaluate the merits of each product and the sales method adopted.

Questions

1 Using the same approach, develop a series of applied tasks for a Sales Manager of a car dealership.

2 Discuss the idea that this type of assessment needs to be tackled in a hierarchical way, i.e. remembering first. In other words, as an assessor should you set up an evaluating task for someone who is currently a novice?

Transfer of learning

Cornford (2002) points out that transfer can only occur after there has been effective acquisition of underpinning knowledge and skills pertinent to the work domain or occupational area. Further, if transfer is the aim, this needs to be done specifically (Stokes and Baer, 1977) as it is not automatic. For the trainer, emphasis is on the learning *process*, on the learner becoming more conscious of their learning pathway, including their capacity to analyse new contexts and find ways in which previous learning can be transferred. Cornford suggests that teachers and trainers need specific guidance on how to bring about this transfer, particularly in the college situation. Transfer from training environments, such as classrooms, to the work environment is a primary aim of any vocational system. Employers state this aim in terms of the worker's flexibility or adaptability.

Cornford (2002) provides a framework for transfer in which he suggests that the trainee is not moved to the next phase until each is satisfactorily achieved:

1 *Assessment at basic skill stage.* Here the trainee becomes skilled at basic level and can demonstrate the skill reliably.

2 *Second practice and assessment occasion.* At this stage the trainee is expected to consolidate skill and basic principles. This may be assisted by asking the trainee to verbalize the steps taken and provide reasoning. This can also be done by the trainer questioning during or after the assessment.

3 *Assessment in a new situation.* Here the trainee is expected to perform in a new situation and demonstrate generalization. Cornford (2002) suggests that the trainer might select the new situation for assessment for this stage.

4 *Generalization.* The trainee should be able to choose the new assessment context for this demonstration of generalization and should produce sufficient evidence to show that generalization has occurred.

5 *Natural work setting.* In this final phase, the trainee is able to demonstrate consolidation and generalization to the more complex environment of the workplace.

As an example, an office skills trainee may learn to use a basic telephone system during the first two phases. The first phase might exclude the customer while the trainee masters the equipment, but the caller should be introduced by phase two. In phases three and four, the trainee would be expected to answer the phone, transfer calls etc. in different simulated environments such as a retail store or call centre, and customers could be internal or external. Numerous practice sessions using different scenarios and phased assessment are much more likely to lead to successful transfer. Again it must be stressed that the learning process is as important as the skill set developed. The trainee needs to be conscious of the ways in which he or she affects the transfer to new and more complex tasks.

Any number of barriers can inhibit transfer and these include:

■ lack of prerequisite language skills or workplace knowledge

■ lack of motivation to participate and learn

- instruction that is irrelevant

- instruction that uses the transmission approach where learners are passive

- inappropriate organizational climate for application of learning.

Caffarella (2002) provides a framework for transfer of learning which covers the people, timing and strategies to be used by the trainer. She goes further to suggest a range of techniques to facilitate learning transfer.

Scaffolding

The metaphor of scaffolding is widely used in educational circles and it refers to the instructor's capacity to assist the learner in the learning process (Wood et al., 1976). This is done by helping the learner to solve problems or accomplish tasks that are just beyond their reach. The ZPD, zone of proximal development (Vygotski, 1962), is explained in the next chapter and it refers the individual's readiness for instruction. In other words, the apprentice learner is only given enough support to progress while continuing to participate and actively engage in the learning process. The task of the instructor is to provide an optimal level of challenge. This involves assisting the learner in the process of articulating problems, making sense, and reflecting. Typically, problems in the realm of customer service have a range of potential outcomes, so that the trainer has to rely on strategies to guide reasoning. This can be problematic as much expertise in customer service is tacit knowledge and the role of the trainer is to make things more explicit. Trainers can use some of the following approaches for structuring:

1 *Organizing work and developing goals*
   Before immersing the learner in the problem-solving exercise, there is a need to establish the goals (which need not be highly specific and can be open ended). The steps involved and timelines for each stage of problem solving may need to be agreed.

2 *Deconstructing the problem/s*
   Before leaping to conclusions, the learner is encouraged to unpack the problem, to identify the parameters and understand fully the context and issues.

3 *Focusing the learner's effort in specific ways*

During the problem-solving process, the learner may need to be provided with support to focus on key issues, so that, in a sense, the trainer is steering the process.

4 *Supervising and prompting*

The trainer can also play a role in supervising the learning process and, from time to time, prompting the learner with facts, models and reasoning that may assist.

5 *Making the tacit explicit*

Throughout the process it may be helpful to encourage the learner to explore tacit knowledge in the field.

6 *Encouraging reflection*

Reflection by the learner on their progress and learning is another key aspect where the process is tracked, reviewed and analysed.

7 *Encouraging transfer*

Having dealt with one problem, the learner is then encouraged to deal with a similar problem. This can be done first with a 'near' problem and then with a 'far' problem.

As one can see from this review of problem-solving as a learning process, the trainer is a facilitator, assisting the individual on a learning journey. The emphasis is on process and the learning can be done in environments in which issues are complex, circumstances changing and solutions varied.

Summary

This chapter has suggested graduated problem-solving as one way to utilize the existing 'know what' and 'know how' of adult learners as the starting point for learning. This approach has the advantage of capturing the many variables at play in each problem situation; it allows learners to draw on their existing experience and schemas relating to customer service and it is located in a specific workplace context. In the ideal situation, the adult learner is solving existing customer relations problems and finding solutions that have a direct organizational and personal impact. In classroom situations, problems provide learners with the opportunity to apply, to do, and to explain why at ever increasing levels of difficulty.

On reflection

This is a very simple problem-solving exercise; however, the aim is to show

how dimensions added to the problem can enhance learning.

Problem

The man with the parrot on his shoulder visits the café every day to buy his take out lunch. On this day, he meets a friend and decides to sit down inside to eat his meal. The parrot makes the occasional vulgar remark. Other patrons are highly amused and entertained by the parrot. Should the man and his parrot be asked to leave?

There are a number of issues around which learning can develop and a few of these are listed here:

- regular customers and their importance to the business
- take out food not to be consumed on the premises as the price is lower based on that assumption, pricing and how it is done
- ambience and entertainment
- pets in restaurants (cultural values)
- dealing with complaints
- food hygiene regulations
- reasons for asking patrons to leave
- how to ask patrons to leave.

This issue could lead to an interesting debate which could then be linked to ideas in the disciplinary area of hospitality such as food hygiene, legal and regulatory issues. A concept map may be useful.

References

Anderson, L.W. and Krathwohl, D.R. (2001) *A taxonomy for learning, teaching, and assessing: a revision of Bloom's taxonomy of educational objectives.* Longman, New York.

Berliner, D. (2005) The near impossibility of testing for teacher quality. *Journal of Teacher Education*, **56**(3), 205–234.

Caffarella, R.S. (2002) *Planning programs for adult learners: a practical guide for educators, trainers, and staff developers*, 2nd edn. Jossey-Bass, San Francisco.

Cornford, I. (2002) Two models for promoting transfer: a comparison and critical analysis. *Journal of Vocational Education and Training*, **54**(1), 85–102.

Dewey, J. (1963) *Experience and education.* Collier, New York.

Knowles, M. (2005) *The adult learner*, 6th edn. Elsevier, Burlington.

McColl-Kennedy, J., Daus, C. and Sparks, B. (2003) The role of gender in reactions to service failure and recovery. *Journal of Service Research*, **6**(1), 66.

Middleton, H. (2005) Developing problem-solving skills. In *Developing Vocational Expertise* (J. Stevenson, ed.). Allen & Unwin, Sydney.

Newell, A. and Simon, H. (1972) *Human problem solving.* Prentice Hall, Englewood Cliffs.

Rogers, C. (1983) *Freedom to learn.* Charles Merrill, Columbus.

Stevenson, J.C. (2003) *Developing vocational expertise: principles and issues in vocational education.* Allen & Unwin, Crows Nest.

Stokes, T. and Baer, D. (1977) The implicit technology of generalization. *Journal of Applied Behaviour Analysis*, **10**, 127–140.

Vygotski, L.S. (1962) *Thought and language.* MIT Press, Cambridge.

Wood, D., Bruner, J. and Ross, G. (1976) The role of tutoring in problem solving. *Journal of Child Psychology and Psychiatry*, **17**(2), 89–100.

8

Sociocultural Perspectives

There are weighty reasons, supported by diverse empirical evidence, for concluding that a gap between skill development outcomes and workplace competence is inevitable. The influence of contextual factors is such that, in actual workplaces, they partly constitute competence. Hence, the learning required for competent workplace performance is normally much greater than the learning that can occur in pre-service courses based on standardized training outcomes. It seems that some context-specific learning, that can occur only from the actual practice of an occupation, is a vital part of competence. Nor is this learning necessarily directly transferable to practice of the same occupation in a different context.

Hager and Smith, 2004, p. 35

Central theme

In the customer service environment in particular, learning occurs more often as a group process than as an individual process. The sociocultural context of the service environment is assumed but should be discussed and utilized during training.

Training implications

1 The climate or organizational culture for customer service needs to be elaborated.

2 The cultural and historical features of customer service can be illustrated by making comparisons with other cultures, other times and other places.

3 Group learning is an important training strategy since service is more commonly provided by a team than by an individual.

4 Where possible, training should occur in a natural situation.

5 Trainees need to join a community of practice (the customer service team) and the trainer's role is to facilitate the movement of the trainee from peripheral to central participation.

6 Transfer of learning is not automatic. Trainers can use a phased approach to facilitate transfer from one context to another.

Introduction

Psychologists tend to analyse people as individuals and study the inner workings of the mind. In this chapter, we will turn to the sociologists who look at how people behave in a social context. The proposition that customer service is culturally and historically situated has been discussed briefly. It is to the concept of context for service that we turn in this chapter, in particular to the sociocultural context of the service environment.

The Australian tourism industry has recently faced something of a dilemma in relation to the service provided to their largest inbound tourist group, the Japanese. No doubt this problem is shared by its main competitor for this tourist market, Hawaii. It appears that the measures taken to providing service for this group do not meet the needs of other Asian inbound groups who are rapidly gaining in terms of numbers of arrivals. Marsh describes the changes made to meet the needs of this market:

> They threw out many of their double beds and replaced them with twin beds because that's what Japanese couples preferred; they put Japanese-speaking staff in the lobby, Japanese food on the menus, slippers in the rooms, and complimentary green tea on the dressing table. Around the streets of Surfers Paradise, Japanese restaurants were built and free-spirited young working-holiday Japanese kids hired to serve. Shops and duty-free stores put up Japanese-language shop signage and hired the same Japanese kids to tout for business. For Japanese visitors to the Gold Coast, the Japanisation of Australia's most famous resort made travel very comfortable indeed (Marsh, 2005).

In something of a backlash, it was later found that Japanese tourists were looking for an authentic Australian tourism experience. Moreover, the other Asian tourists arriving from Korea, Indonesia, Thailand and China had different priorities to the Japanese and were likewise looking for an Australian cultural experience, a 'G'day' from downunder.

Customer service is linked closely to the culture of the country, organization and workplace. In this example, attempts were made to replicate the culture of the inbound tourist group. Culture is a system of shared beliefs, values, customs, behaviours and artefacts that the members of society use to communicate with their world and with one another. Culture is usually invisible to those immersed in it as they take normal standards of behaviour for granted.

For a trainer, the use of contrast is an effective way to highlight differences in culture, in customer service in practices of greeting, personal presentation, attentiveness, questioning and solving problems, to name just a few explicit cultural indicators. The aim of this is not, as it was in the early example, to imitate (in some cases so badly that it offends) a culture, but to develop an awareness and sensitivity to the sociocultural context.

Communities of practice

The trainer, too, must recognize that their teaching is part of a sociocultural framework. Current conceptualizations of sociocultural theory draw heavily on the work of Vygotski (1962) who describes learning as being embedded within social events. This is referred to by other theorists as *situated* learning (Lave and Wenger, 1991). Not only is learning situated, learning occurs in a community of practice. Each of these communities has unique characteristics. According to Lave and Wenger (1991) communities of practice are self-organized groups of people who share a common sense of purpose, a desire to learn and know what each other knows. The customer service team thus needs to be committed to the joint relationship and needs to work and learn as a team. In doing so the group develops shared meanings and ways of doing things.

At the risk of using too many tourism examples, let us look at the idea that a tourism experience is *unique*. A search of 'unique tourism experience' on Google produces over 10 000 hits. For this experience to be unique for the customer, service must vary from country to country, from place to place and from person to person! This is in contrast to the homogeneous customer service provided by the major franchises and hotel groups where you get the same greeting whether you are in London or Vancouver. Thus, determining the delineation of a community of practice in a global economic environment is an interesting consideration.

Here are some slogans pitched at customers that demonstrate shared meanings within a customer service community of practice:

- You're in great hands with us

- We have a heart

- Service excellence guaranteed

- We aim to please

And some pitched at staff:

- Own the problem, own the customer. Lose the problem, lose the customer. It's that simple

- If you're not serving the customer, you'd better be serving someone who is

- Always give people more than they expect

- Marketing is people, not just numbers

- Give the customer a good reason to come back

- Yeah, we've got that

- Can do!

Clearly, these slogans do not indicate any kind of service differentiation. Readers are reminded of the Hilton Hotel initiative mentioned in Chapter One where their style was described as 'intuitive'. More sophisticated organizations work towards developing a cohesive community of practice in which members participate in a well defined workplace culture. This culture makes a valuable contribution to brand awareness, in this case the brand being Hilton Hotels.

Customer service culture

Creating a customer service culture can be approached in a structured way, such as the eight steps suggested by Morrow (1995, 2006):

1 Management must make the measurement of service quality and feedback from the customer a basic part of everyone's work experience.

2 Be very clear about specifying the behaviour that employees are expected to deliver, both with external customers and their coworkers.

3 Explain why giving excellent customer service is important.

4 Create ways to communicate excellent examples of customer service both within and outside the company. Institute celebrations, recognition ceremonies, logos and symbols of the customer service culture and its values. This is where you want the mugs, buttons and banners. Have a customer service bulletin board to feature service incidents that were special.

5 Indoctrinate and train everyone in the culture as soon as they are hired.

6 Encourage a sense of responsibility for group performance.

7 Establish policies that are 'customer friendly' and that show concern for your customers. Eliminate all routine and rigid policies and guidelines.

8 Remove any employees who do not show the behaviour necessary to please customers.

However, another approach to point five would be to take a much more organic approach to training, one which is more open-ended, allowing for organizational learning and responsiveness to marketplace trends. Some of the perspectives and training approaches of this chapter can be used to create a service culture which encourages full participation and allows learners to take ownership of the learning process.

Training approaches

With the concept of situated learning in a community of practice in mind, trainers could look more closely at learning that occurs in a natural situation in which the learner communicates and collaborates with others. This is a wonderful aspiration for trainers, that they facilitate learning by immersion of learners in an appropriate natural context. The ultimate aim for vocational training is that the learner is assimilated into the community, in this case into the community of the workplace. While this is an ideal to strive for, it is somewhat problematic in some workplaces, for example retail stores, where trainees are often part-time and transient. They are also isolated behind cash registers most of the time.

This ideal is also problematic for the teacher working in a college, for example, training apprentice hairdressers or network support engineers.

Indeed, it is argued by some that the opportunity to leave the context of the workplace to study in a training room provides another type of valuable learning experience, away from what has been described as the 'hot action'. In this environment, there is the opportunity to learn about new concepts and reflect on action. In this chapter, we will look at critical incident analysis, brainstorming and conversational learning. However, before doing so, it is timely to re-visit the context for service and try to articulate what it looks like in a more explicit way.

Describing the context

In Table 8.1, a number of context dimensions have been developed and then linked to examples of simple and complex instances of communication with customers. This is for illustrative purposes only, an exercise that may be undertaken in any service enterprise or industry.

The following variables may be some that impact on consumer decision-making and therefore reflect the context for customer service provision.

Customer profiles

Otherwise known as market segments, customer profiles help the service enterprise to identify the needs of customers most likely to purchase the goods and services provided. Some service based businesses work with a limited range of customers (such as child care centres), while others work with a wide scope of profiles as they attract customers of all demographics, including some visitors from overseas (such as a museum or theme park).

Emotional state of the customer

In the helping professions, there are many service roles in which people assist others in the most difficult of circumstances. Emergency response teams, critical care nurses and lifeline counsellors are just a few examples. At the other end of the continuum, there are those who deal with customers who are enjoying themselves, at dinner, a nightclub, bar or cruise. Sometimes these customers enjoy themselves far too much! In most other situations, such as supermarkets, customers are rarely at an emotional extreme, unless the queues have been too long.

Duration of the service encounter

In some situations, the service encounter is fleeting, for example paying for petrol or dropping a coin in a booth attendant's hand (no doubt soon to be mechanized). In other circumstances, the relationship with the service provider is a long one. Doctors, physiotherapists and tour guides spring to mind. Here, too, there is a difference between a short visit over a period of months, and a three-week wilderness tour where you are together with your customers from eyes open to eyes shut. Indeed, although not listed here, other customers are another feature of the service landscape. On tours these interpersonal relationships need careful management.

Number of variables in the customer decision process/product dimensions

How much help does the customer need? Is this a simple decision (full cream or lite?) or a complex decision involving any number of elements such as purchasing a motor car or real estate? This can also refer to the number of product dimensions. Some products are simple while others have a range of features where assistance is needed to select the most appropriate of these, as one would with a new sound system.

Significance of the purchase decision

Linked to the previous dimension, the customer will weigh some decisions much higher than others. A car is a long-term and expensive purchase and therefore something to be agonized over. Likewise, the choice of wedding planner. On the other hand, these things are relative, a child spending pocket money weighs various considerations quite carefully.

Competing demands

In most service environments, there are competing demands, phones ringing, people waiting and e-mails to respond to. Some customers are in a hurry, others more than happy to take their time.

Social and cultural features of the service environment

Some service environments need to be highly authentic or fit with a theme. It would not be appropriate for someone selling eco-tourism adventures to use non-recyclable products or for a cultural festival to misrepresent one of the cultural groups participating. In some service enterprises, the ambience is absolutely integral to product development.

Relative importance of customers

Where a business is reliant on repeat business, customer loyalty is essential. Other service businesses rely instead on passing trade and can focus on high volume at the expense of personalized service.

Physical work environment

The cramped and hot conditions of kitchens are legendary for the stress that is then communicated to floor staff, and in turn to restaurant customers. Some workplaces are temporary, such as festivals and special events.

Clarity of work roles

In some cases, work roles are very clearly delineated, in others everyone does a bit of everything. Bank tellers are expected to know a lot about products and procedures and be able to answer questions well beyond their primary roles. In small businesses, the roles are often very blurred.

Policy and procedure

Sometimes policy and procedure are very clear and employees are required to comply in every instance. In others, policy does not exist, in yet others, employees are expected to solve problems, working with and around the policy framework.

Business and legal framework

Linked to the above considerations, service providers must be mindful of duty of care and fair trading principles. Pressure for sales can lead to unethical sales practices.

These dimensions are shown in Table 8.1 on the left hand side and they are illustrated with examples on the right. Similar dimensions could be developed for any service industry rather than tourism and hospitality illustrated here. They could also be developed for a specific enterprise and the service that it offers.

Table 8.1 illustrates ways in which training off the job can help learners to make sense of what happens on the job. This type of table, which illustrates a continuum of difficulty, also enables the trainer to provide case studies at increasing levels of complexity. There is nothing special about this table, it is a table that any group of trainers could develop to match the context of their industries and workplaces and thus highlight some implicit factors that contribute to the complexity of what they do every day. In the last chapter, the concept of scaffolding was introduced. The table developed here as an example could also provide the trainer with a scaffold on which to base concept development, with different dimensions and different levels of complexity. While the temptation for most trainers is to simplify and offer solutions, this approach is a much more expansive and open-ended one. In addition to scaffolding, the trainer needs to think about *problematizing*. This is a process of challenging the learners who may be trying to reduce a problem and oversimplify the issue. Problematizing complex learning is discussed by Rieser (2004, p. 288):

> This focus of resources inherent in problematizing can address the problems of nonreflective work and superficial analysis, encouraging and requiring students to address critical questions and ideas in the discipline . . . . By leading students to encounter particular ways of thinking, scaffolding can provoke students, 'rocking the boat' when they are proceeding along without being mindful enough of the rich connections of their decisions to the domain content.

Thus, the trainer is treading a fine line structuring and problematizing. However, this approach can assist learners to become more attuned to their service environments and more explicit about their reasoning.

In summary, the idea that training is 'situated' in specific contexts and cannot be divorced from workplace practice suggests that concepts and theoretical principles need to be applied in realistic and authentic social settings. The focus also shifts from the individual as a learner to group learning where shared meanings are negotiated through collaboration and interaction. In such training, a multitude of variables or dimensions are at play and the trainer's role is to make those variables explicit and encourage learners to use them in problem-solving

Table 8.1 Contextual dimensions for customer service decision-making

Context dimension	Low ⟵⟶ High	
Customer profiles, market segments	Consistent, known, e.g. regular café customers, same orders	Variable, unpredictable, e.g. cruise ship clients
Emotional state of customer	Unemotional, e.g. pensioner ordering a sandwich	Fatigued or elated, e.g. delayed passenger/bridal couple
Duration of service encounter	Short, transient encounter, e.g. restaurant customer paying bill	Lengthy, continuous customer relationship, e.g. Contiki tour group
Number of variables in customer decision process or service provision	Few variables to consider, e.g. overnight booking for a motel	Highly technical or complex, e.g. convention booking 5000 delegates
Competing demands	Quiet, ample time, single customer, e.g. Bed and Breakfast morning meal	High level, multiple customer demands, e.g. checkout peak simultaneous group departure and arrival
Significance of customer's decision (perception)	Insignificant, low relative 'cost', e.g. takeaway coke order	Risk level high, expense high, important decision, e.g. Commonwealth Games bid
Social and cultural features	Limited value inputs, e.g. free city bus route	Values motivate product/service, e.g. indigenous cultural tours, eco-tourism educational tours
Relative importance of customers to business survival	Transient customers, loyalty not vitally important for survival, e.g. train station fruit juice bar	Customer is crucial to business success or failure, e.g. signing of event naming rights sponsor
Physical work environment	Stable, well equipped, e.g. five star hotel	Temporary, ill defined, potentially unsafe, e.g. community event
Clarity of work roles	Singular role, independent, e.g. coffee cart operator	Shared responsibility for customer, team reliance, e.g. dive adventure
Policy and procedure	Simple policies, rules, procedures, e.g. fast food hygiene practices	Complex policy, multiple procedures, empowered to vary, e.g. travel agency group reservations
Business environment and legal context	Low risk, low competition, e.g. tourism information office	High risk, multiple legal implications, safety risk, e.g. adventure tourism

Source: Van Der Wagen, 2006, p. 94

exercises. However, if one was to do this at the beginning, the novice learners might well be overwhelmed by the multitude of disparate cues. The role of the trainer is to plan a curriculum, a graduated series of learning experiences that enable classroom trainees to transfer learning from the cool action of the training room to the hot action of the workplace.

In order to bring about transfer, a concept associated with scaffolding is fading. Fading is the process of removing support so that the learner is independent. As Cornford (2002) highlighted in the previous chapter, transfer requires specific attention on the part of the trainer. This phase of fading is an integral part of the process, ensuring that the learner is able to rely on his or her own frameworks and has achieved mastery.

Critical incident analysis

Critical incident analysis, whether conducted formally or informally (as often occurs at coffee breaks) can contribute in highly effective ways to solving workplace problems and can lead to learning that is personal and immediately relevant. Both positive and negative incidents can be analysed, some theorists suggesting that starting with a positive incident is a useful approach.

- Focus on an incident which had a strong positive influence on the result of the interaction and describe the incident

- Describe what led up to the incident

- Describe how the incident helped the successful completion of the interaction

It is usual to request two or maybe three such incidents, but one at least should be elicited. When this has been done, the procedure is repeated but now the group is asked to focus on incidents which have led to inadequate service and to follow the above formula to place the incidents in context. Additional questions can include:

- Why do I view the situation like that?

- What assumptions have I made about the customer/problem/situation?

- How else could I interpret the situation?

- What other action could I have taken that may have been more helpful?

- What have I learned about my practice?

- What have I learned about my profession?

There are, of course, incidents that will not be productive in terms of learning, as it is unrealistic to expect that every incident will lend itself to this type of analysis. Some need to be allocated to the 'life's like that' basket. Indeed, a cautionary note is in order. The tone of the discussion is vitally important as critical incident analysis can lead to assigning blame and attribution error (a tendency to blame people rather than circumstances). Some individuals may perceive that they have made mistakes that they might otherwise be unaware of and take this very much to heart even where this is expressed in the most subtle of ways. The level of trust, empathy and collaboration in the group is crucial to its success. Use of critical incident technique (CIT) as an educational tool should be a group or team activity. Regular meetings should be held to discuss incidents, positive and negative. There should be a focus on system improvement rather than individuals in a 'no blame' culture.

In practice

The value of critical incident analysis as an educational tool and its relationship to experiential learning:

Experiential learning and teaching strategies, designed to facilitate this, have become popular in nursing and midwifery education in recent years. It is advocated that such learning enables the development of knowledge, skills and attitudes grounded in practice through the use of reflection on action. One strategy that may be utilized by nursing/midwifery educators to develop reflective ability in both themselves and students is critical incident analysis. It is suggested that critical incident analysis has value and is appropriate for developing interpersonal skills and self-awareness. It is proposed that critical incident analysis is a valuable educational tool which enables nursing/midwifery students to draw on past experiences and make sense of them, not only facilitating learning from clinical practice but also going some way towards bridging the gap between theory and practice (Parker and Bar-On, 2000, p. 111).

Questions

1 It could be suggested that workplace critical incident analysis is commonly practiced in the tea room or around the water cooler. Can you recollect an informal process of incident analysis?

2 Discuss the potential benefits of critical incident analysis when managed formally with learning as the intentional outcome.

3 Debriefing highly complex and problematic issues is not to be taken lightly. Discuss the role of the facilitator in managing such a session.

4 When is a training facilitator out of his or her depth in this type of situation and how should this be managed?

Brainstorming

Brainstorming is another widely used training technique, traditionally managed to encourage the development of ideas. The facilitator of a brainstorming session needs to be mindful of the following guidelines:

- Participation: everyone in the group should be encouraged to participate and no criticism should be allowed as this inhibits creativity, people should suspend judgment

- Quantity: large numbers of divergent ideas should be allowed

- Unusual ideas: while some ideas seem bizarre they should be encouraged, new perspectives are valued

- Recording: ideas should be recorded, traditionally this is done on a whiteboard but there is software available which can harness everyone's ideas simultaneously

- Facilitation: the degree to which boundaries are established is monitored by the facilitator who may devise the purpose for the session, develop questions as prompts, or encourage particular lines of development.

For brainstorming to work effectively, participants should feel that there is progress along a path and a degree of resolution to a problem or issue. The alternative is a messy conglomerate of random ideas. A brainstorming session that aims to enhance service systems and procedures needs some level of negotiation and agreed outcome. For learning to occur, a skilled facilitator needs to draw on the experience of the participants and assist the group to articulate their decision-making processes in the final stages of the brainstorming session.

Conversational learning

The concept of dialogue has had a place in educational theory since the times of Plato and Socrates. Dialogue with question, answer, challenge and response, debate and discussion have all had their place in training rooms and classrooms. This approach is much more unstructured than most. In some circumstances, the trainer has an agenda and, to some extent, leads the conversation. However, in most cases, the participants also bring new knowledge and new perspectives to the conversation. This leads to co-construction of knowledge, a valuable concept in the complex field of customer service. It is important, however, to point out that sometimes conversation is simply communication, it does not lead to meaningful learning on the part of the individuals or the group. Conversational learning can however provide a meaningful pathway to learning:

> The proximity of group members links experience through both status and solidarity based on the course of conversation. This occurs regardless of whether the conversation occurs between individuals in face-to-face interaction or through technology. The role of the OD/HRD professional in conversational learning focuses on creating space for conversation, inviting different voices into the conversation, and cultivating a safe space for deliberation about difficult but meaningful issues (Baker et al., 2002, p. 204).

Critical incident analysis, brainstorming and conversational learning are suggested here as possible approaches to training that is relatively unstructured, closely linked to everyday issues, relevant to participants and open-ended in terms of outcomes. Many theorists suggest that this organic approach is more suitable to the modern organization which is characterized by constant change, described by Hager and Smith as 'the new workplace' (Hager and Smith, 2004, p. 39). In addition, cooperative learning straegies have been demonstrated to foster critical thinking, problem-solving, enhanced self-esteem, interdependence and individual accountability (McInerney and McInerney, 2005).

Summary

Sociocultural theories stress that learning is situated. Most adult learning, described as informal learning, occurs in social settings such as family and workplace. While recognizing this, the trainer often needs to extend the learner into new communities. In this case, the community is generally a specific workplace, or in the case of college education, a vocational occupation such as building or nursing. It may be helpful also to consider service providers as a community of practice (Lave and Wenger, 1991). Many economies are increasingly dependent on service provision and not enough attention is given to understanding what this means.

CASE STUDY

Our mission

Our mandate is to protect the community through the notion of working together and developing meaningful partnerships.

Our vision

Our Police Service is dedicated to:

- the safety and security of our community

- working cooperatively with the members of our community and

- supporting our members personally and professionally.

Our values

The Police Service believes in:

- partnership with the community: the police and the community share in the responsibility for crime control and public safety

- dedication to public service, diversity and quality of the workforce; therefore, we seek to recruit and retain individuals who possess those qualities

- collaboration with neighbourhoods better to understand the nature of local problems and to develop meaningful and cooperative strategies to solve these problems

- teamwork, mutual respect, and cooperation so that the community can be served

- enhancing the skills of all police to ensure motivation, creativity, dedication and professionalism, while creating an atmosphere of job satisfaction, enthusiasm, security and personal career development

- education and the use of current technology assist us in determining and meeting the needs of our growing community

- positive community relations and being an integral part of our community

- maintaining the highest ethical and professional standards and

- being a diverse and non-discriminatory police service.

Our community policing philosophy is:

- To move in the direction of implementing a problem-oriented policing organization.

- To move as rapidly as possible to include the community as an active partner in problem-solving and crime prevention.

Questions

1 Describe the workplace culture to which the Police Service aspires.

2 What do you think a 'problem-oriented policing organization' is?

3 As the Director of Training and Development for this Police Service, what approach based on the concept of *situated learning* would you take to achieving this culture in the organization?

4 Can you describe the work context of police work with a focus on the variables that contribute to the level of complexity of this work (similar to Table 8.1)?

5 How would you handle *transfer* of skills/knowledge and prior experience of new recruits into this Police Service so that these employees become part of the established culture of this workforce?

References

Baker, A., Jensen, M. and Kolb, D. (2002) *Conversational learning: an experiential approach to knowledge creation.* Quorum Books, Westport.

Cornford, I. (2002) Two models for promoting transfer: a comparison and critical analysis. *Journal of Vocational Education and Training*, **54**(1), 85–102.

Hager, P. and Smith, E. (2004) The inescapability of significant contextual learning in work performance. *London Review of Education*, 2(1), 33–46.

Lave, J. and Wenger, E. (1991) *Situated learning: legitimate peripheral participation.* Cambridge University Press, Cambridge.

Marsh, R. (2005) *All Asia ain't the same.* Inbound Tourism Studies Centre, viewed April 2005 <http://www.inboundtourism.com.au/article_seven.html>

McInerney, D.M. and McInerney, V. (2005) *Educational psychology: constructing learning*, 4th edn. Pearson Education, Frenchs Forest.

Morrow, P. (1995) *Customer service: the key to your competitive edge.* Advantage Plus Books, Houston.

Morrow, P. (2006) *Customer service: how to do it right!* Advantage Plus Books, Houston.

Parker, J.D.A. and Bar-On, R. (2000) *The handbook of emotional intelligence: theory, development, assessment, and application at home, school, and in the workplace.* Jossey-Bass, San Francisco.

Reiser, B. (2004) Scaffolding complex learning: the mechanisms of structuring and problematizing student work. *Journal of the Learning Sciences*, 13(3), 273–304.

Van Der Wagen, L. (2006) Vocational curriculum for Australian service industries: standardised learning for diverse service environments? *Journal of Hospitality and Tourism Management*, 13(1), 85–96.

Vygotski, L.S. (1962) *Thought and language.* MIT Press, Cambridge.

9

Activity Theory

A third way of considering the patterns of learning we have observed is through activity theory, in particular through the notion of expansive learning articulated in the context of workplace learning by Engeström (2001). In activity theory, as in this study, the focus is on the social and organizational context rather than on individual learning and contradictions (or atypical events) as sources of change. Engeström (2001) draws attention to what he calls horizontal or sideways learning and development in which problem solving occurs essentially through interactions among peers without resort to a conventional knowledge hierarchy. This is a potentially useful way of conceptualising the learning pattern we have identified as 'dealing with the atypical' in which there is no set procedure or process and learning is required to address a problem or contradiction in ways which lead to an acceptable outcome.

Boud and Middleton, 2003, p. 201

Central theme

Activity theory provides a model of complex action. The object, for example 'quality service', is not static but dynamic. Learning is a process of expansive development, taking into account the perspectives of the participants, such as employees, customers, supervisors and community. Mediating artefacts, such as computer software, policy manuals and language, play an important part in mediating meaning.

Training implications

1 Object-oriented action, in this case the object being 'customer satisfaction', needs to be elaborated by example as being situated in a rich and complex environment.

2 By initiating discussion about what 'customer satisfaction' means using examples, the trainer can illustrate that solutions are partial, points along the way. The concept is dynamic.

3 Use of mediating artefacts and their role in communication is an essential part of training. The learner should be more conscious of the roles played by these artefacts in mediating communication. In particular, technological changes are profoundly influencing many customer service interactions.

Introduction

As the chapters in this book progress, frameworks get more and more complex. This final model is challenging; however, it provides some valuable insights for the customer service trainer frustrated with simple formulas for multifaceted training problems. The steps for complaint handling spring to mind as an overly simplistic approach. How many trainers have listed the following steps, elements in financial services competency unit 'Resolve Customer Complaints', on a slide?

1 Identify customer complaint issue

2 Record complaint/dispute

3 Refer complaint/dispute

4 Implement corrective action policy regarding customer complaints

5 Process complaint

6 Follow up

To make matters worse, in some training rooms, the ability to list the sequence correctly leads to a satisfactory assessment! The most useful concept introduced in this chapter is the idea that each complaint resolution is unique and that the concept of customer satisfaction is dynamic.

Activity theory

Activity theory is a model of artefact-mediated and object-oriented action developed by Russian theorist Vygotski and his colleagues in 1962. This 'new psychology' does a great deal to capture the richness of workplace practice. For example, customer service can be seen as *an object which is socially and culturally defined by service provider, employer and consumer*. A Russian colleague of Vygotski's, Leont'ev, introduced the concept of work as a division of labour, performed as a collective activity, this, too, reinforcing concepts of work as interactions between human beings and their environment. Change management in organizations is a topical issue which also has implications for employee training and development. Where an organization is growing, changing and also learning in response to environmental factors, there needs to be an approach which accommodates this level of adaptation. This chapter will look at learning from the viewpoint of the individual, the work group and the organization. It will consider a wide range of external and internal environmental variables. It will consider the language and other mediating artefacts of the communication environment that impact on customer service. Most importantly, 'good customer service' will fit with this model as something organic and evolutionary. In some organizations, new customer initiatives are experiments, they are exploratory and the customers' reactions often unexpected. At the cutting edge of technology based customer service, the pace of change is extraordinary. Training in this context cannot present service as a simple and static concept.

Activity theory is deeply contextual and seeks to understand specific local practices; it is based on a dialectical theory of knowledge focusing on the creative potential of human cognition; and it is developmental bringing about changes in human practices. Engeström (1999, p. 384) proposes an expansive learning cycle or spiral. According to the author:

> The process of expansive learning should be understood as construction and resolution of successively evolving tensions or contradictions in a complex system that includes the *object or objects*, the mediating *artefacts*, and the *perspectives* of the participants.

The value of this theoretical approach is in the description of problem finding as part of the ongoing reconstruction process, with solutions at best partial, described as 'arbitrary points along the way' (Engeström, 1999, p. 381).

With this in mind, a model developed by Engeström (1987) is adapted here to show customer service in banking as the object of activity, with relevant mediating artefacts such as manuals, texts, concepts and tools such as computer software.

The object

As Figure 9.1 illustrates, the activity system model can be used to analyse the customer service environment by identifying 'appropriate' customer service as the object (which is dynamic and socioculturally defined).

Subject

The subject in this example is the employee. However, an employee does not act unilaterally, he or she is in a community.

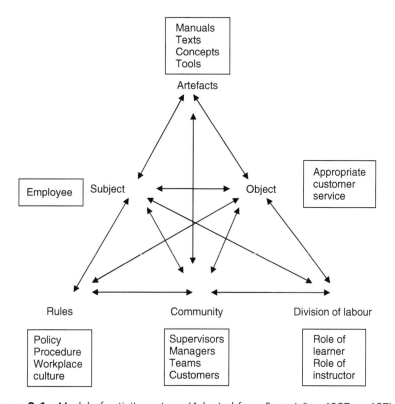

Figure 9.1 Model of activity system. (Adapted from Engeström, 1987, p. 187)

Community

Community for the employee includes colleagues, team members, supervisors and, of course, the customer/s.

Rules or conventions

The conventions that cover the banking industry in this example include separate counters for transactions and enquiries. The latter is the counter where staff are able to handle more difficult questions. In the most extreme situation, the employee may call on the assistance of the manager, another member of the community. Another convention of most banks is the process for customers to make formal written complaints. The culture of the workplace may be that employees are disempowered and thus call the manager on most occasions or there may be subtle pressures to avoid bringing problems to the attention of more senior staff, hoping that they will go away.

Artefacts

Language is an artefact, terminology such as a 'joint account' mediates the communication. Trainers can improve the quality of training by developing an understanding of the various mediating artefacts in the workplace such as manuals, texts, concepts, tools and symbols which are used to establish the service ethos. In the banking sector, the artefacts are likely to include manuals, software, banking products (different types of account) and concepts such as online banking. In a restaurant, the menu is an artefact that has a vital role to play in mediating communication between the server and the customer, as well as between the server and the chef. In many industries, the computer plays a mediating role in communication as the service provider is constrained by the options available on the screen.

Division of labour

In our banking example, the division of labour could be the role of the trainer and the trainee. Is the trainer using a telling style of instruction? Is the trainer using a facilitation style where the onus is on the trainee to participate more fully in learning? Furthermore, fewer and fewer routine bank transactions are conducted personally and the role of the bank teller is changing to that of the bank seller.

Social cognition learning

The social cognition learning model asserts that culture is the prime determinant of individual development. Therefore, following this approach, an employee's learning is affected by the workplace culture in which he or she is placed. According to the social cognition learning model, workplace culture teaches employees what to think and how to think. Learning and development occurs informally as experiences are shared with peers and superiors. In the early period of employee socialization, induction and training are used to acclimatize the individual and from that point on most learning is informal and experiential.

Language is a primary form of interaction through which the organization transmits its service vision, both formally and informally, to its employees. The rich body of knowledge that exists in the culture is passed on to newcomers. Some of this knowledge is positive (how to work efficiently) and sometimes it is negative (how to rip off the business). Language and culture transmission from the wider social environment is also influential. This learning is internalized over time as interactions with the surrounding culture and the people involved (including customers) grow.

When we talk about instruction, clearly the most valuable instruction and assessment is in the zone of proximal development, which is the stage at which an individual's skills can be developed with the assistance of others. Individuals construct their understanding of new knowledge at different rates and in different ways from each other. There is no 'one size fits all' approach to effective instruction (McInerney and McInerney, 2005). In organizations where there is high staff turnover, this means that there are employees at all stages of development in understanding and expertise at any given time. This would point to the need for careful assessment of individual training needs and development potential. It would also explain why traditional information based training sessions lead to limited learning transfer into the job environment.

In practice

The history of banking provides an illustration of a customer service revolution. From early days of coinage (where the coin 'was worth its weight in gold') to modern day online banking, the industry continues to ramp up the range of products and increase accessibility to these products. In the UK, there are about 6.5 million online customers, in the USA around 22 million.

Consider briefly the history of modern banking (although we must acknowledge the early history of banking in China and Ancient Europe):

1700s	■ Largely centralized banks, issued own bank notes, dealt with merchants
	■ Started lending, cash credit (early form of overdraft)
	■ Mainly commercial, growing branch networks

1800s	■ Savings banks for all levels of the population, interest paid on savings
	■ Emerging personal banking, growing retail branch networks
1900s	■ Emergence of the credit card, cheque and savings accounts for individuals, wide range of products, home loans and insurance
	■ Division between retail banking and investment banking
2000s	■ Move from paper money to electronic money
	■ Online banking, call centres for product information and problem-solving
	■ Closing or reducing size of many bank branches
	■ Reliance on ATMs and retailer use of EFTPOS

Questions

1 In light of this relentless process of change to service provided by banks, discuss the pros and cons of online banking.

2 Using the model provided in Figure 9.1 of the activity system, describe the system that delivers service to you as a customer.

3 Discuss the concept of the 'object' of quality customer service as a dynamic as opposed to a static outcome.

Activity theory and learning

Stevenson (2003) uses activity theory to derive principles that might guide vocational learning. These principles are:

■ to proceed from the learner's sense of vocation

■ to situate learning in concrete, functional, purposive settings

■ to focus primarily on the capacity-to-do

- to engage in understanding interrelationships in learning/working activity systems

- to share meanings

- to relate meanings so derived to other activity systems and the wider community

- to build connections among meanings and different renditions of meanings, together with a facility of operating upon such interconnections (Stevenson, 2003, p. 44).

Constructivism is a philosophy of learning founded on the premise that, by reflecting on our experiences, we construct our own understanding of the world we live in. Learning is thus most relevant and useful when it addresses the issues that are most appropriate for the learners. This approach also stresses the importance of models, or mental frameworks that assist the learner to construct his or her meaning. Learning is not just a process of remembering facts. The process of learning, or construction of meaning is vitally important.

Constructivism emphasizes experiential learning, making connections and developing new understandings. It involves analysing and interpreting and it includes internal as well as external dialogue. In this framework learning is active and experiential.

Graham Hendry (1996) lists seven constructivist principles and their teaching applications. These should be considered in the light of what makes an effective instructor.

Principle 1: Knowledge exists only in the minds of people. In the classroom, knowledge exists in the minds of students and the teacher, not on the blackboard, in books, on disks, in teacher or student talk or in the activities that teachers and students devise.

Principle 2: The meanings or interpretations that people give to things depend on their knowledge. Teachers and students give meaning to instructional materials according to their existing knowledge and may, therefore, generate different meanings for the same materials and experiences.

Principle 3: Knowledge is constructed from within the person in interrelation with the world. Teachers or teaching methods *per se* do not change students' ideas; rather, change or construction occurs from within, through students' interrelation with the world of which teachers are a part. Students do not simply absorb transmitted knowledge.

Principle 4: Knowledge can never be certain. There are no absolutely right or wrong answers or ideas, only ones that are more or less useful and sustainable. Thus, all knowledge can be reconstructed and should be continually open to re-examination.

Principle 5: Common knowledge derives from a common brain and body which are part of the same universe. Individuals share the same brain processes and body characteristics and inhabit the same world and can construct common knowledge through their discussion of solutions to the same problems. Despite the individual nature of the construction of knowledge, this knowledge construction is based upon common biological processes (such as perception) across humans. This knowledge will reflect the biological and experiential maturity of the individuals.

Principle 6: Knowledge is constructed through perception and action. In particular, learning is facilitated by active involvement in problem-solving and conflict resolution.

Principle 7: Construction of knowledge requires energy and time. Individuals are most motivated to construct knowledge in non-threatening, supportive and challenging learning environments. The construction of knowledge is promoted by encouraging students to discuss, explain and evaluate their thoughts within a social context.

(Adapted from McInerney and McInerney, 2005)

Mass marketing and customization

At the tough end of the services spectrum the customer is sovereign. He or she expects a uniquely customized product and this includes both goods and services. In many ways this problematizes customer service training because one is moving into a realm in which judgment is paramount. This being the case, training is no longer standardized and the solutions are open-ended.

Indeed, with the Internet as a tool to select products, many mass market choices are being handled online by the customer. This includes booking airline flights as an example. It is only where complex and customized products are needed that the customer resorts to using an expert, in this case a travel agent. Thus, the shift to online purchasing further reduces the need for formulaic training, since the simple transactions are often made on computer. In the future, high end personal service provision will involve extensive product knowledge and sophisticated analysis of customer needs and expectations. These days, the travel agencies no longer earn commissions on bookings but instead earn service fees. This is likely to be replicated in other sectors of the service economy. Where the customer is paying for something as intangible as 'pure service', expectations are high. This framework offers the opportunity for trainees to heighten their awareness of the complexity of service provision, and for them to understand that solutions are often ever evolving approximations. It certainly changes the traditional roles of instructor and learner, moving away from didactic methods of instruction to more interactive, constructivist approaches.

Summary

Periods of change in the organization, when for example marketing to emerging new customer segments, provide the ideal context for moving employees from cruise control to adopting new perspectives and approaches. Many organizations introduce new products, re-brand themselves, identify new markets and introduce new procedures. In all these situations, perspective taking is an imaginative approach to the training components of change management.

CASE STUDY

In their article, Egan and Shipley (1995, pp. 812–813) discuss the competitive nature of the UK banking industry and stress the importance of differentiation and customer orientation:

> In recent years, there has been a dramatic increase in the number and quality of new entrants into the UK financial services sector, an intensity of rivalry which has impacted upon all the sub-sectors examined in this research. The dynamics of the competitive environment in the merchant

banking sector – particularly its global nature – have clearly encouraged companies within it to develop a differentiated, focused approach to their market. The firms in this sector scored highly on all measures of customer orientation and placed much greater emphasis on the quality of service delivery than the other sub-sectors studied. The merchant banks emerged as the most customer-oriented of the four sub-sectors, and a more detailed examination of the multiple-item scale components demonstrated a much closer approximation of literature-prescribed best practice than building societies, banks and insurance companies.

There is evidence within the data that banks, building societies and insurance companies are becoming increasingly aware of the importance of developing a customer orientation. Despite this, a deeper investigation of the full range of items measured suggests a tendency towards marketing myopia and a particularly strong vulnerability to attack from specialist rivals. Attempts at being all things to all people normally end with firms not being anything special to anyone at all. The current consolidation within these sub-sectors of the financial services industry will give only short-term relief to the combined effects of deregulation, market liberalization, technological innovation and market entry from foreign rivals and non-traditional sectors. In this context, the marketing challenge has only just begun and the belief in customer orientation now needs to progress towards a more structured approach to market segmentation, the development of appropriately tailored products and a fundamental re-evaluation of service delivery systems.

Questions

1 'The person who used to be a bank teller is now a bank seller'. Discuss this statement.

2 What is a service delivery system?

3 Using a model or framework describe the service delivery system of a housing loan to a banking customer.

4 Can banks be described as learning organizations?

5 What are the implications of using a framework such as that provided by activity theory as the basis for training in banks?

References

Boud, D. and Middleton, H. (2003) Learning from others at work: communities of practice and informal learning. *Journal of Workplace Learning*, **15**(5), 194–201.

Egan, C. and Shipley, D. (1995) Dimensions of customer orientation: an empirical investigation of the UK financial services sector. *Journal of Marketing Management*, **11**, 807–816.

Engeström, Y. (1987) *Learning by expanding: an activity-theoretical approach to developmental research*. Orienta-Konsultit Oy, Helsinki.

Engeström, Y. (1999) Innovative learning in work teams: analysing cycles of knowledge creation in practice. In *Perspectives on Activity Theory* (Y. Engeström, R. Miettinen and R. Punamaki, eds), pp. 377–405. Cambridge University Press, London.

Engeström, Y. (2001) Expansive learning at work: toward an activity theoretical conceptualization. *Journal of Education and Work*, **14**(1), 133–156.

Hendry, G.D. (1996) Constructivism and educational practice. *Australian Journal of Education*, **40**(11), 19–45.

McInerney, D.M. and McInerney, V. (2005) *Educational psychology: constructing learning*, 4th edn. Pearson Education, Frenchs Forest.

Stevenson, J.C. (2003) *Developing vocational expertise: principles and issues in vocational education*. Allen & Unwin, Crows Nest.

Vygotski, L.S. (1962) *Thought and language*. MIT Press, Cambridge.

10

Zen and Mindfulness

Mindfulness is both radical introspection and direct connection with the phenomenal world. It is not simply inward looking. It is more a matter of being fully present in every step of life. By attempting it we throw into relief all the obstacles in our minds which prevent us making direct contact with experience. Simple degrees of mindfulness are immensely valuable, indeed essential, at all levels of personal growth.

Brazier, 2001, p. 73

Central theme

Being highly attentive, noticing elements that are novel, immersing oneself in the present and leaving existing mental schemas (including stereotypes) behind, can lead to a state of mindfulness. This approach to customer service training is most relevant for experienced employees who need new perspectives. The use of probabilistic language can further contribute to responsiveness to a range of customers and contexts.

Training implications

1 By providing stimulus training material, such as images, cartoons, videos or demonstrations, the trainer can facilitate perspective taking.

2 Learners can be encouraged to leave their mental schemas behind, to immerse themselves in the present and notice elements that are novel.

3 Previous, recent experience can also be used for perspective taking and analysis.

4 Pre-service and post-service briefings lend themselves well to this approach.

Introduction

The essence of Zen is attempting to understand the meaning of life directly, without being misled by logical thought, or language. Zen is about living in the present with complete awareness. Mindfulness, a Zen concept, is being grounded in the present, actively attending to stimuli and leaving past thinking and mental schemas behind. In the Western world, mindfulness emphasizes active cognitive processes, it promotes 'contingency responsiveness' (Murray, 1998). In contrast, Eastern meditation focuses on stilling thought and is a much more passive process. In this chapter, mindfulness will be used as a construct as it was originated by Langer (1947, 1989). A mindful person is open to new perspectives and relinquishes old thought patterns (including stereotypes). In contrast, a mindless person is tied to old thought patterns, is on automatic pilot, lacks empathy and is closed to new perceptions. Langer (1947) suggests that mindfulness, as a state of mind, has three key qualities: creating new categories, being open to new information and being aware of more than one perspective.

Langer (2000) defines mindfulness and mindlessness:

> Mindfulness is a flexible state of mind in which we are actively engaged in the present, noticing new things and sensitive to context. When we are in a state of mindlessness, we act like automatons who have been programmed to act according to the sense our behaviour made in the past, rather than the present. … We are stuck in a single, rigid perspective and we are oblivious to alternative ways of knowing (Langer, 2000, p. 29).

Training in cross-cultural awareness generally attempts to open up these rigid perspectives and challenge assumptions. This can be done well, in which case service providers are more flexible and responsive, or it can be done badly so that stereotypes of cultural difference are further reinforced. The best approaches develop awareness of different customer perceptions and thus greater empathy on the part of the provider. This is consistent with the theme of this chapter of leaving preconceptions behind, being more conscious of customer cues and more aware of customer responses.

Langer (2000) suggests that there are three myths about learning:

1 The basics should learned so well that they should become second nature

2 To pay attention to something we should hold it still and focus it

3 It is important to learn how to delay gratification.

When people learn mindfully, they are more likely to accommodate change than people who get trapped in routines. Secondly, it is easier to pay attention to something if novel things are noticed, thus rather than fading, the item becomes more stimulating. Finally, Langer argues that learning mindfully engages the learner in such a way that reward and gratification are not necessary: 'mindful learning engages people in what they are learning and the experience tends to be positive' (Langer, 2000, p. 31).

In his book, titled *Zen Therapy*, David Brazier (2001) talks about getting out of the box of preconditioned feelings to become open minded and open hearted. He likens this to the self-actualization force discussed by humanist psychologists such as Carl Rogers. As he suggests, this idea allows people to move away from narrow, mechanistic ideas towards a psychology that makes room for human potential:

> As we grow, we experience. As we experience, we learn. As we learn, we run the risk of encapsulating ourselves in a shell of set views, the dead bones of experience past. Within our armour of views we start to put our trust in security. We are then affronted by the vicissitudes of life which disturb our illusions. Zen, as therapy, aims to help us hatch out of our shell and experience the world again fresh and new (Brazier, 2001, p. 34).

Applying these concepts at the superficial level of customer service training may seem absurd. However, since customer service interactions make up almost all of their working lives for the majority of the workforce, it is worth considering this idea of openness, particularly with regard to other people around us. The focus moves away from the self, toward the present and to those around us. Such a philosophy has implications for effective interactions with others in which aspects of emotional intelligence are brought to bear. In this context, Ciarrocchi and Godsell (2006) have developed strategies for developing mindfulness-based emotional intelligence.

The practice of meditation is well known, and Brazier uses it to enhance mindfulness. He suggests sitting still, paying attention to the breath to settle the mind, and sometimes focusing on imagery. In an introduction to a training session I undertook in Canada some years ago, we were privileged to participate in a smoke ceremony run by the indigenous Canadian leaders of the region. This formal introduction to the conference and to each workshop had the benefit of focusing on the present, while acknowledging the spirits of the earth, the water and the sky. In participating in this ceremony, all involved were asked to clear their minds and to be more receptive in workshops they were about to attend. This authentic ceremony, using smoke as a metaphor, brought about a higher level of attentiveness, greater participation from the audience, and a more meaningful learning experience. Readers who have attended many lectures and workshops with their thoughts many miles away, on the past, the future and anything but the present, would appreciate this.

A practitioner in customer service training might consider a similar exercise with a focus on slowing down and becoming attentive in the present and this could be helpful if done appropriately. However, this experience needs to be authentic and it is not suggested that novice trainers start to develop or imitate opening ceremonies or indeed lead meditation if inexperienced in this field.

Mindfulness using conditional language

In her research, Murray (1998) demonstrates that students can be taught the principle of enhancing immediacy and can apply this to everyday communication. Learners can also be taught to engage with uncertainty which promotes contingency responsiveness. In her model, shown in Figure 10.1, Murray shows

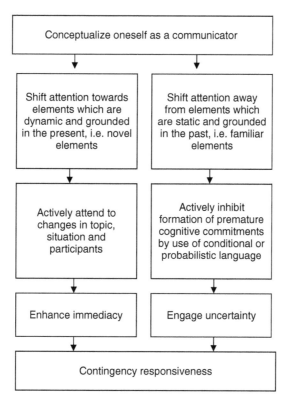

Figure 10.1 Mindfulness in communication model (Murray, L., 1998. Reproduced with permission)

how learners can actively attend to novel elements in communication and inhibit premature cognitive commitments by using conditional or probabilistic language. By achieving a higher level of contingency responsiveness, learners can improve their communication effectiveness.

As Murray (1998) points out, she would not present the model to learners, but rather use training techniques of encouraging feedback and discussion as part of the discursive pattern in the classroom. In particular, she works with conditional or probabilistic language, using words like as 'could', 'might' and 'possibly'. In her study, she uses cartoons to teach learners how to be more mindful in their communication. The example that follows illustrates how this might work using a cartoon depicting customer service.

Pre-training

The woman doesn't understand anything about cars and the frustrated mechanic is trying to explain why it will cost a lot to fix it. He says it may be beyond repair as it is old and out of condition. It was not serviced regularly. The woman feels helpless, she has had no experience with car repairs and doesn't understand what he is telling her. She is upset that she will lose her car that she has been driving for years and wants to blame him for his shoddy work.

Post-training

The mechanic *might* be telling his customer why he cannot repair her car right away. He *may* be using technical language that she doesn't understand. He *appears to be* concerned. The woman looks quite passive, but that *could be* because she can't join in a technical conversation about her car's engine. Both people are looking at the car, so there is *probably* no conflict, just agreement that the problem is serious. He is holding a spanner but this is not used to point or demonstrate aggressively. Their body language *seems* to show that they share the same concern. One perspective *could be* that he too has no idea what is wrong.

Brazier (2001) suggests that in Zen, 'it is common for what could be called shock tactics to be used to jolt the mind out of its ruts' (p. 41) and this idea is useful in the service sectors in which organizations need to stay abreast of changes in consumer needs. Many employees, particularly those with long years of service, become caught up in mindless routine and are often less and less attentive to new customer cues. These ideas support the idea that trainers could use photographs, scripts of conversations or video footage as the stimulus for 'jolting the mind'. Better still, briefing and debriefing (before and after service periods in which mindfulness is practiced) could be part of the training design. By seeing small details, problems and issues can be more easily resolved. This is because they are not couched in global terms, such as 'we were understaffed' but, instead, expressed as 'station ten had too many tables for the breakfast service period', which is more easily remedied. The primary purpose of this approach is for employees to develop acute observation skills and to make suggestions for improvements to products and procedures as a result of their observations. This contributes to organizational learning – these ideas are brought together, discussed in groups and actioned.

In practice

An empirical test of the service-profit chain in a large UK retail business explored how employee attitudes and behaviour can improve customer retention and, consequently, company sales performance. Data were collected from 65 000 employees and 25 000 customers from almost 100 stores. The business collected customer satisfaction for just under 1 year and employee attitude data using the same questionnaire for 2 years. Four data sets were judged suitable outcome indicators for exploring the relationship between customers and employees: cash sales figures, absence data, staff turnover, and customer complaints. Staff turnover and customer complaints data were unrelated to the other major outcomes variables in the dataset. A case study attitude chain was developed from the statistical model created as a result of analysis. Perceptions of line management were strongly related to perceived company culture, which was strongly linked to employee commitment. Employee commitment acted on sales through three routes: directly on sales, mediated through customer service satisfaction, and through reduction in staff absence. The study demonstrated the significant role of human resource management in the service sector, because of the importance of a positive organization culture, good line management, employee commitment, and employee attendance to the effective working of the service-profit chain.

Questions

1 Explain your experiences with service staff working on auto-pilot.

2 How does this study link effective human resource practices to outcomes for the organization?

3 Training is not mentioned here. How does training play a role in the management of human resources?

4 While many long-serving employees may need to become more attentive, for many organizations the issue is quite different. Their employee turnover is so high that there is barely time to train people before they leave. Discuss.

Stereotyping and customer service

There can be no doubt that cultural stereotypes are evident in customer service encounters (Phizacklea and Miles, 1980; Ramirez and Härtel, 2001). Stereotyping is typically described as defining one's expectations of particular groups or individuals based on categorization. Some common descriptions might include:

- simplified and fixed image of all members of a culture or group

- generalizations about people that are based on limited, sometimes inaccurate, information

- predictions about customers based on incomplete information about their country of origin, culture, race or social class

- single statement or attitude about a group of people that does not recognize the complex, multidimensional nature of human beings.

All of the above descriptions imply that stereotyping is bad, particularly the last description highlighting the multidimensional nature of human beings. Stereotyping can be unhelpful if it is applied mindlessly. However, in many situations stereotyping also helps to categorize customers and allows service staff to assist them more readily. Consider for example, a family with very young children. It is a fairly safe bet that the family has limited time for shopping or dining out and that speedy service will be appreciated. Indeed, marketing professionals spend most of their working lives on the process of defining market segments (customer groups) and tailoring products to meet their needs. All these products have a service component. Stereotyping, in the sense of grouping like customers and anticipating their needs based on previous experience with similar customers, is thus part of everyday business for many service professionals. However, there are of course limitations and stereotyping can have profoundly serious consequences for customer communication. In the worst case scenario, the customer is able to make claims for discrimination based on the relevant legal acts.

In a study of how stereotypes affect customer service, Ramirez and Härtel (2001) found that:

■ service quality was of a higher standard when providers were serving persons from a similar background

■ openness toward dissimilarity was significantly related to managers' ratings of provider service performance

■ there is an association between the stereotyping carried out by the employee and the service provided in terms of behaviours such as tone of voice, non-verbal communication (specifically avoidance descriptors), amount of small talk, helping initiatives etc.

The second of these findings supports the application of mindfulness in communication training. While stereotyping cannot be entirely avoided, nor should it be as it can contribute to service efficiencies and customer satisfaction, service providers need to be very aware of the use of stereotyping as a shortcut in the customer encounter. As described in this study, openness toward dissimilarity should be a highly sought after attribute in employees, particularly those providing service to international visitors or a diverse customer base. Aguilar and Stokes (1995) provide valuable suggestions for developing multicultural awareness and sensitivity in customer service.

Perspective taking

This approach involves perspective taking and this can be encouraged in training. In a customer transaction, the perspectives are those of the service provider, the customer, customers in the vicinity, colleagues and the supervisor. All might see a situation differently. For example, if a customer were holding up the line by having a conversation with the cashier, this could be frowned upon by several of the people described. On the other hand, the customer could be a regular who has just had a serious health problem diagnosed. There may be some justification for the extra time taken even when others are waiting. In training, all of these perspectives can be explored using probabilistic language.

Employees 'who sleepwalk through their day' (Langer and Moldoveanu, 2000) are acting mechanically and mindlessly. They cannot contribute to ongoing quality improvement as they are not attentive to the work situation, to change and to new possibilities. There is competitive advantage for an organization whose employees are responsive to change. Furthermore, mindless employees do not attend to the customer. They do not offer a greeting, they do not look for non-verbal cues and they do not listen. In many cases, customers expect conversation as part of the transaction, particularly when shopping or eating out. Using mindfulness, a trainer can disturb (in a constructive way) employees who are in a rut, who are on automatic pilot and oblivious to customers' particular or unique needs.

One must consider, however, that this construct cannot be used as the basis for training on every occasion. There are specific training situations in which it is appropriate, in others not. Novice employees needing to adjust to new workplace routines would be out of their depth if they practiced mindfulness and were constantly hyper-attentive to novel elements. In contrast, employees who have been with the organization for a period of time could benefit dramatically from this approach. It could move them from a plodding mindset to one in which they are receptive to new ideas, developing a heightened awareness of customer service contingency factors.

In their book on managing the unexpected, Wieck and Sutcliffe (2001) devote a chapter to managing mindfully. Their argument is based on the premise that most organizations share a diet of the unexpected and that in order to respond to this they need to 'reliably forestall catastrophic outcomes through mindful attention to ongoing operations' (Wieck and Sutcliffe, 2001, p. 22).

Summary

Periods of change in the organization, when for example, marketing to emerging new customer segments, provide the ideal context for moving employees from cruise control to adopting new perspectives and approaches. Many organizations introduce new products, re-brand themselves, identify new markets and introduce new procedures. In all these situations, perspective taking is an imaginative approach to the training components of change management.

CASE STUDY

The first photograph shows a training session.

1 Would this room setup contribute to a learning experience consistent with the themes of this chapter?

2 If you were running training for a group of employees with the intention of developing mindfulness in customer service, how would you design the training and what type of environment would you use for training? Make some assumptions about the organizational context.

The second photograph illustrates a service situation.

1 Describe the service context in every detail.

2 Discuss the needs of this customer using probabilistic language.

3 From this exercise develop a list of three things you would pay more attention to if you were working in a children's hospital and wanted to improve customer service.

References

Aguilar, L. and Stokes, L. (1995) *Multicultural customer service.* McGraw-Hill, Burr Ridge.

Brazier, D. (2001) *Zen therapy, a Buddhist approach to psychotherapy.* Robinson, London.

Ciarrochi, J. and Godsell, C. (2006) Mindfulness-based emotional intelligence: research and training. In *Linking emotional intelligence and performance at work: current research evidence with individuals and groups* (V. Druskat, F. Sala and G. Mount, eds), pp. 21–52. Erlbaum, New Jersey.

Langer, E. (1947) *The power of mindful learning.* Perseus Books, Cambridge.

Langer, E. (1989) *Mindfulness.* Perseus Books, Cambridge.

Langer, E. (2000) Mindful learning. *American Psychological Society*, **9**(6), 29–32.

Langer, E. and Moldoveanu, M. (2000) The construct of mindfulness. *Society for the Psychological Study of Social Issues*, **56**(1), 1–9.

Murray, L. (1998) *A study of mindfulness in communication skills training.* University of Technology, Sydney.

Phizacklea, A. and Miles, R. (1980) *Labour and racism.* Routledge & Kegan Paul, London.

Ramirez, A. and Härtel, E. (2001) *How do stereotypes affect the ability to deliver good service in the hospitality industry?* Monash University, Caulfield.

Wieck, K. and Sutcliffe, K. (2001) *Managing the unexpected: assuring high performance in an age of complexity.* Jossey-Bass, San Francisco.

11

Conclusion

One size does not fit all

As this book has progressed, the role of the trainer has varied. In parts, the role has been that of the traditional instructor, who follows a transmission model of teaching, with a focus on outcomes. In other parts, the book has reviewed perspectives that change the role to that of facilitator. Here, the learning can be described as unstructured or organic and the role looks more like intervention than training. These perspectives are helpful to us in service environments as there are some circumstances in which training follows a formula (many organizations are renowned for the quality and consistency of their training which is highly job specific) while, in others, 'customer service' is extremely hard to define. In professions, such as nursing and policing for example, the scenarios that people deal with every day are extremely complex and many require imaginative solutions in response to customer needs. In yet other organizations, the product is multifaceted and the customers are spending vast amounts of money. In these contexts, service cannot be formulaic and decision-making is heuristic. As Lin and Darling (1997, p. 198) point out:

> the organizational learning analysis should lead to a change in corporate culture. Moreover, employees' perceptions of customer service training are undergoing significant change: notably from viewing such training as an indoctrination tool to seeing it as a genuine investment in the future of both the individual and the company.

There are simply no super-solutions for the customer service trainer. For the most part, training prepares people for tricky, complicated and challenging solutions. For this reason, training has to fit the needs of the organization and the learner.

Innovation in customer service training

Increasingly, organizations are looking at concepts such as the learning organization and are investing in organizational development more seriously. According to Peter Senge (1990, p. 3) learning organizations are:

> organizations where people continually expand their capacity to create the results they truly desire, where new and expansive patterns of thinking

are nurtured, where collective aspiration is set free, and where people are continually learning to see the whole together.

When these ideas are linked to the provision of quality service, a new focus is needed. One needs to look at process rather than 'skill' development. Total quality management is an example of an approach that is process-oriented with incremental change in response to changing economic, business and consumer environments.

Earlier in this book, the characteristics of service were identified. Highlighted was the fact that interaction with customers is variable as it is based on interpersonal communication. So it should be, the expectation is that the service provider is responding to the client's needs. Why buy a drink from a dispensing machine when a little repartee with a bartender would be more interesting? Lin and Darling (1997, p. 195) provide an interesting model for what they call a 'processual analysis of training'. They suggest that customer service training should be studied as a multidimensional issue, recognizing the following three dimensions:

- Analytical – tasks, technique, procedure and system

- Behavioural – attitudes, perceptions and motivation

- Organizational – management style, corporate culture, structure and communication flows.

Their model is illustrated in Figure 11.1 and it shows how all three dimensions need to be attended to simultaneously.

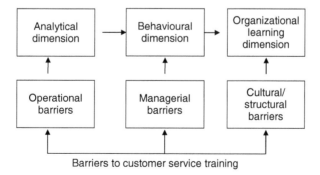

Figure 11.1 An initial processual analysis of customer service training (Lin and Darling, 1997, p. 195)

These authors continue to suggest that the following five components are necessary for organizational learning:

- a learning imperative
- shared vision
- cross-functional teamwork
- open-mindedness
- experience sharing.

Careers in training and education

A career in human resource management, organizational development, training or education is rich and varied. In the same way that service providers are responsive to customer needs, trainers need to be responsive to the needs of industries, organizations, groups and individuals. Chappell (2003, p. 3) calls this constructive alignment, that is 'the appropriateness of particular pedagogical strategies to the different purposes and settings in which contemporary vocational, workplace and organizational learning takes place'. There is thus a wide range of practices in adult education, teaching and learning that occurs in classrooms, in training rooms and on the job. Some training takes the form of direct instruction (most induction or orientation programmes fit this mould), while other training is experiential and is facilitated by a mentor. In the latter situation, learners take much more responsibility for their learning progress and can self-assess against goals and outcomes. In the ideal situation, the outcomes produced suit the needs of the individual, the work team and the organization. However, in other situations, the learning may be personally relevant but of limited value to the organization in the short term. The philosophy and policy of the organization towards personal and professional development is part of a human resources plan. Some organizations have short-term utilitarian views, while others embrace and encourage learning in almost every sphere.

Beckett and Hager (2002) provide examples from aged care to illustrate the diversity of behaviour of residents with dementia:

Competence is then the inference from a diversity of evidence, via judgement of fitness, rightness and appropriateness. Such judgements are saturated with values, and in that way, they are not only context bound, but culturally driven ... Skills are socially located and advanced when their significance is apparent. Integrated competence gives prominence to this social location and to the location of the individual within that social location. That is why context specific judgements are intended to be integrable and organic. The whole person is a fairly specific setting and is more likely to demonstrate an authentic competence than a behaviouristic, but context-free, tabulation of technique (sometimes called 'tick n flick' or 'check-listing') (Beckett and Hager, 2002, pp. 57–58).

As the chapters of this book have suggested, an integrated and sophisticated whole-organizational approach to customer service training is necessary. Bringing in a dynamic trainer for a day-long session in a training room is unlikely to lead to transfer to the job or long-term organizational learning. Issues around customer service are linked inexorably: product development, sales and marketing, policy, procedure, recruitment, selection and training, to name just a few. Where organizations are service oriented, marketing and human resource management strategies (including training and development) need to work in tandem.

References

Beckett, D. and Hager, P. (2002) *Life, work and learning: practice in postmodernity.* Routledge, London.

Chappell, C. (2003) Changing pedagogy: contemporary vocational learning. *OVAL Working Papers*, viewed 12 September 2006 <http://sitesearch.uts.edu.au/oval/publication_result.lasso>

Lin, B. and Darling, J. (1997) A processual analysis of customer service training. *Journal of Services Marketing*, 11(3), 193–205.

Senge, P. (1990) *The fifth discipline: the art and practice of the learning organization.* Random House, New York.

Appendix A

Sample Generic Competency
Units and Elements

Australian National Training Authority (GCS01)
Generic guideline units – Customer service

Executive summary

There is considerable variation in how customer service is defined, as a result of its meaning being contingent upon a range of factors including the role of the worker, context, enterprise and industry. While a universally accepted definition of 'customer service' remains elusive, few can dispute that customer service is a critical area of competence needing to be addressed by any enterprise seeking to grow in future competitive markets. High performing companies share a set of basic operating principles. Among these are to 'stay close to the customer' as well as a capacity 'to motivate their employees to produce high quality and value for their customers'. The Guideline Customer Service Competencies constructed and described in this document are based on two pieces of independent, although complementary, research followed by a comprehensive national validation process. Both the research efforts and the validation process involved extensive consultation across a wide range of industries.

Guideline elements

A total of 27 elements were identified as having relevance across a range of industries. The 27 elements are listed below. Some of the customer service competencies inevitably will be perceived as crossing boundaries into other disciplines such as strategic planning, marketing, sales, front-line management, database management etc.

Fifteen of the 27 elements, in combination with one or more other element(s), form natural growing points for the construction of customer service units of competency. They are termed here 'primary' elements, and are as follows:

Primary elements

P01 Establish contact with customers

P02 Present a positive organizational image

P03 Handle customer feedback

P04 Record customer feedback

166

P06   Respond to complaints

P07   Refer complaints

P08   Identify customer needs and expectations

P09   Provide the identified customer needs and expectations

P14   Contribute to quality customer service standards

P15   Implement customer service systems

P17   Assist customer to articulate needs

P18   Satisfy customer needs

P22   Analyse needs of customer populations

P23   Plan and develop customer service

P24   Evaluate customer service relationship

The above 15 elements of competency are 'supported' by another 12 elements. These 12 elements, according to the research, are unlikely to be considered as foundations for units of competency, but can build well onto primary elements. These elements of competency, thus termed 'support' elements, are listed below:

Support elements

S05   Maintain personal presentation standards

S10   Develop knowledge for a specified range of products and services

S11   Manage unmet customer expectations

S12   Direct customers with unmet needs

S13   Respond to changes in customer needs

S16   Implement team customer service standards

S19   Lead customer service team

S20   Manage networks to ensure customer needs are addressed

S21   Exercise judgment to resolve customer service issues

S25   Develop customer service systems

S26   Initiate customer service improvement

S27   Promote the business to customers

These Customer Service guideline elements serve only to establish minimum competency requirements. They may be contextualized by an industry, an industry sector or a company. Contextualization can add detail and change terminology and provide examples to relate more directly to an industry context. An acceptable form of contextualization would be changes in language to reflect industry usage. For instance, some industries may want to refer to customers as 'clients' or 'patients'. Removing, or altering the intent or outcome of the guideline elements is not contextualization – it is a new element and cannot be linked to the guideline element.

Primary elements

P01 Establish contact with customers

- Welcoming customer environment is created and maintained.

- Customers are acknowledged and greeted courteously and politely according to enterprise policies and procedures.

- Communications with customers are clear, concise and courteous.

- Appropriate communication channels are used.

- Rapport/relationship with customer is established and a genuine interest in customer needs/requirements is expressed.

- Effective service environment is created through verbal and non-verbal presentation according to enterprise policies and procedures.

P02 Present a positive organizational image

- Information is provided to the public to maintain organization's image and accountability.

- Professional ethics are maintained to enhance customer commitment and to build return customer base.

- All actions taken are in keeping with the required organizational image.

P03 *Handle customer feedback*

- Customer feedback is promptly recognized.

- Customer feedback is handled positively, sensitively and politely.

- Information regarding problems and delays is promptly communicated to customers and followed up within an appropriate timeframe as necessary.

P04 *Record customer feedback*

- Description of communication between customers and organization is completed accurately and in simple language.

- Any further records required to support feedback are prepared, monitored and stored according to organizational procedures and policies.

P06 *Respond to complaints*

- Complaints are processed in accordance with organizational procedures established under company policies, legislation or codes of practice.

- Necessary reports relating to the complaints are obtained, documented and reviewed.

- Decisions are made, taking into account applicable law, company policies and codes.

- Resolution of the complaint is negotiated and agreed where possible.

- A register of complaints/disputes is maintained.

- Customer is informed of outcome of investigation.

P07 *Refer complaints*

- Complaints that require referral to other personnel or external bodies are identified.

- Referrals are made to appropriate personnel for follow-up in accordance with individual level of responsibility.

- All documents and investigation reports are forwarded.

- Appropriate personnel are followed up to gain prompt decisions.

P08 Identify customer needs and expectations

- Customer preferences, needs and expectations are clarified.

- Special requirements of customers are identified promptly and advice provided on relevant products/services.

- Communication appropriate to the relationship and the purpose of the interaction is used.

- External assistance is accessed as required.

P09 Provide the identified customer needs and expectations

- Knowledge of specified products/services is applied to provide assistance to customers.

- Alternative products/services are suggested if necessary.

- Features and benefits of relevant products/services are explained to customers.

- Special promotions for products/services are suggested to customer according to organization policies.

- Confirmation is sought from customer that needs, and where practical, expectations have been satisfied.

P14 Contribute to quality customer service standards

- Customer service standards are accessed, interpreted, applied and monitored in the workplace in accordance with enterprise policies and procedures.

- Contributions are made to the development, refinement and improvement of service policies, standards and processes.

P15 Implement customer service systems

- All personnel are encouraged consistently to implement customer service systems.

- Customer feedback is reviewed in consultation with appropriate personnel and is analysed when improving work practices.

- Customer service problems are identified and adjustments made to ensure continued service quality.

- Adjustments are communicated to all those involved in service delivery within appropriate time frames.

- Delivery of services/products is coordinated and managed to ensure they effectively and efficiently meet agreed quality standards.

P17 Assist customer to articulate needs

- Customer needs are fully explored, understood and agreed.

- Available services/products are explained and matched to customer needs.

- The rights and responsibilities of customers are identified and effectively communicated to the customer as appropriate.

P18 Satisfy complex customer needs

- Possibilities for meeting customer needs are explained.

- Customers are assisted to evaluate service/product options to satisfy their needs.

- Preferred action is determined and prioritized.

- Potential areas of difficulty in customer service delivery are identified, and appropriate actions are taken in a positive manner.

P22 Analyse needs of customer populations

- Information is sourced through both formal and informal channels.

- Information on issues related to the business environment that affect customers is collected and utilized in assessment.

- Information is analysed and interpreted to identify and assess customer needs, expectations and satisfaction levels.

- Decisions about the matching of services and customer needs are based on up-to-date information.

P23 Plan and develop customer service

- Plans are developed to meet customer and organizational needs and to improve customer service.

- Specific aspects of product/service and their delivery are modified as needed to meet changing customer service requirements.

- Competitive comparisons are analysed and evaluated as input into the planning process.

- Customer service provisions are established through detailed and structured market research and analysis.

- Changes to customer service are within organizational ability, i.e. policies and budgetary framework as well as procedural and legislative requirements.

P24 Evaluate customer service relationship

- Information that measures customers' level of satisfaction with its products/services is obtained.

- Information on how the organization compares with competition and best practice is analysed and evaluated.

- Appropriate initiatives are implemented or actioned.

Support elements

S05 Maintain personal presentation standards

- Self-confidence and appropriate communication is used to project a good image of the organization.

- Impact of presentation on different types of customers is considered and made according to the organizational policies.

- Specific presentation and representation requirements for particular work functions are satisfied according to organizational requirements.

S10 Develop knowledge for a specific range of products and services

- Features and characteristics of a specified range of products/services are identified and described accurately.

- Knowledge of a specified range of products/services, including comparisons between specified products and services, is developed and maintained.

- Enterprise manuals, labels and instructions are read, interpreted and stored according to enterprise policies.

- Availability of products and services is determined according to enterprise and/or supplier information.

S11 Manage unmet customer expectations

- Unmet expectations are established.

- Barriers to satisfying expectations are identified.

- Information as to why expectations cannot be met is advised to customer according to organizational policies and procedures.

- Enquiries requiring additional information are prioritized, recorded and responded to with the shortest possible delay.

- If the enquiry is a complaint, complaints procedure is followed according to organizational policies.

S12 Direct customers with unmet needs

- Unmet customer needs are identified.

- The suitability of other products/services is discussed with the customer to minimize potential loss in areas of products/services.

- Recommendations and referrals are undertaken within the scope of the area of responsibility according to organizational policies and procedures.

- The customer is supported to make contact with other services according to organizational policies and procedures.

- All advice to customers about available services is consistent with current relevant legislative and statutory framework.

S13 Respond to changes in customer needs

- Changes in customer needs are identified and assessed.

- Changes are negotiated with customers and other relevant parties.

- Records of changes in client needs are maintained as required and according to organizational policies and procedures.

- Strategies to respond to changes in customer needs are implemented within a customer service plan.

S16 Implement team customer service standards

- Team and work activities are planned and implemented to meet customer needs and expectations and minimize inconvenience.

- Resources required to undertake team tasks while meeting required customer service levels are identified.

S19 Lead customer service team

- Coaching/mentoring is used to assist colleagues to deal with customer service issues and achieve the ultimate service potential.

- Team is motivated to achieve high standard of service to customer.

- Team is informed on changes in policies and procedures, which impact upon their relations with customers.

- Team is provided with regular feedback in regard to achievement/non-achievement of standards of customer service.

- Team members are encouraged to contribute feedback in regard to achievement of customer service.

- Training is undertaken as required to meet changing needs.

S20 Manage networks to ensure customer needs are addressed

■ Effective regular communication is established with customers.

■ Relevant networks are established, maintained and expanded to ensure appropriate referral of customers to products/services from within and outside the organization.

■ Procedures are put in place to ensure that decisions about targeting of customer services are based on up-to-date information about the customer and the products/services available.

■ Procedures are put in place to ensure that referrals are based on the matching of the assessment of customer needs and availability of products/services.

■ Records of customer interaction are maintained in accordance with organizational procedures.

S21 Exercise judgment to resolve customer service issues

■ Implications of issues for the customer and for the organization are identified.

■ Appropriate options for resolution are analysed, explained and negotiated with the customer.

■ Viable options proposed are in accordance with appropriate legislative requirements and enterprise policies.

■ Matters for which a solution cannot be negotiated are referred to appropriate personnel.

S25 Develop customer service systems

■ Procedures are put in place to promote consistency and adherence to organizational standards and procedures when dealing with customers.

■ Strategies and mechanisms are developed and implemented to ensure that all relevant customer information is collected, maintained, stored and accessible to relevant personnel.

■ Opportunities for feedback by customers are provided.

- Feedback is sought on an ongoing basis.

- Methods of improving customer service are analysed and recommendations made to appropriate personnel.

- Procedures are put in place to ensure staff have ready access to up-to-date and relevant information about the range of services available to customers.

S26 Initiate customer service improvement

- Information is analysed and suitable means of improving customer service identified and actioned.

- Suitable recommendations to appropriate personnel for improvements are developed and communicated.

- Procedures and documentation are put in place to ensure staff have access to additional specialist information and assistance when assessing customer needs.

- Reports and feedback in accordance with company requirements provided and communicated.

S27 Promote the business to customers

- The competitive position of the business is enhanced through its promotion and goodwill.

- A plan for promoting the business to customers is developed, benchmarked and implemented.

- Mechanism for regular review of the promotion plan is established.

- Required alternative promotion strategies are implemented, managed and maintained.

Source: Copyright Australian National Training Authority, ANTA (reproduced with permission).
  Available from National Training Information Service
http://www.ntis.gov.au/cgi-bin/waxhtml/~ntis2/std.wxh?page=80&inputRef
=602 (accessed 19 April 2005).

Appendix B

Negotiating a Learning Contract

What is a learning contract?

A learning contract provides the learner with an opportunity to decide, in consultation with the trainer, how assessment will take place. In most learning situations you have experienced in the past, trainers will have created assignments for you, told you what to do, how to do it and how you would be assessed. This is an opportunity for you to decide (within the boundaries of the unit) what you would like to do, how you would like to do it and how you will be assessed.

Some learners immediately welcome this opportunity as they have burning issues and interests which they would like to pursue, questions they would like to ask, or activities they would like to undertake. Others are slower to warm to the idea, never having experienced such a high level of autonomy. However, once accustomed to the idea, learners discover that the learning contract gives them, for the first time, real ownership of their learning. The level of interest is higher as the topic chosen is highly relevant. Learning becomes a pleasure, a source of interest and satisfaction.

The learning contract should not be a stumbling block, it is simply a means to an end, allowing you to provide your own evidence for assessment. As you can imagine, it is important that you and your trainer agree on the form the evidence will take. There is no single way to draw up a learning contract, as many of them are as individual as the learners themselves.

The best way to negotiate a learning contract is to begin with a copy of the competency unit and brainstorm some ideas. You need to be very careful that what you decide to do is achievable within the time available. It is generally true that learner projects of this nature soon get out of control as many learners are unrealistic in their assumptions about how much work is involved. It is far better to do a thorough job than to take on more than you can manage. Remember: you must be *realistic* about what can be achieved in the time available. An example of a learning contract is shown on the next pages. It is not essential that yours follows exactly the same format.

Learning Contract

Name: Balin Banizir   Due Date: 12 November 2004
Assessment Project: Explore history of the indigenous people in the local area with a view to providing information to visiting overseas hotel guests.

Main features: Investigate a range of sources, collate information, present to a group.

THHGCS01B/01   Develop local knowledge

Develop local knowledge	Investigation	Presentation
1.1 Identify and access appropriate sources of information on the local area	✓	
1.2 Record and file information for further use as appropriate and in accordance with enterprise procedures	✓	
1.3 Identify and obtain the types of information commonly requested by customers	✓	
Update local knowledge		
2.1 Identify and use opportunities to update local knowledge	✓	
2.2 Share updated knowledge with customers and colleagues as appropriate and incorporate into day-to-day working activities		✓

Tasks to be undertaken for assessment

1 Sources of information have already been identified – see below.

2 Relevant information will be collated and organized.

3 Information will be discussed with other learners.

4 One page summary will be submitted with a folder of relevant information.

Books/texts

■ Aboriginal Support Group – Manly Warringah Pittwater, A Story to Tell ... On a Road Toward Reconciliation: *1979–2000: An Account of the First Twenty-One Years of Life and Work of the Aboriginal Support Group – Manly Warringah Pittwater*, Narrabeen, ASG-MWP, 2002.

- Foley, Dennis, *Repossession of our Spirit: Traditional Owners of Northern Sydney*. Photography by Ricky Maynard, Canberra, Aboriginal History Inc., 2001.

- Hinkson, Melinda, *Aboriginal Sydney: A Guide to Important Places of the Past and Present*. Photography by Alana Harris, Canberra, Aboriginal Studies Press, 2000.

- Lee, Emma, *The Tale of a Whale: Significant Aboriginal Landscapes of the Northern Beaches*, Dee Why, Warringah Council, 2002.

- Wood, Nancy, *Nobody's Child*, Narrabeen, ASG-MWP, 1999.

Library resources

Visit to Warringah Library Service, Pittwater Library and Manly Library.

Aboriginal Heritage Office

Contact Aboriginal Heritage Manager, Warringah, Willoughby, Lane Cove and North Sydney Councils.

Signed learner: _____   Signed assessor: _____   Date: _____

Steps in negotiating your learning contract

Select your area of interest

For each of the competency units, there are likely to be one or two areas which you find particularly interesting or relevant. You may, for example, be planning to start your own business and might want to learn about the success of various recruitment strategies used by service organizations.

Decide on your learning needs

You need to know what it is you will achieve in terms of meeting your personal learning needs. There is little point in researching an area about which you know a great deal. You need to identify a key area which will be relevant to your career development in the next five or ten years. You are expected to cover the topic broadly from a theoretical point of view, even if your study has a fairly narrow focus. Use this as an opportunity to learn something new.

Check on the relevance of your area of interest

You might like to review some current literature including books, trade magazines and newspapers. Talking to industry personnel and staff who share similar interests in the subject area could also be productive. It will give you great satisfaction to produce a report which has relevance to industry.

Decide on work placement

You need to decide whether to undertake this project as research (contacting a range in industry personnel), as industry placement, or as part of your normal employment. As pointed out earlier, this is a unique opportunity to gain access to key personnel in senior positions. It would be a great shame to waste this opportunity.

Decide on your learning objectives

This is an appropriate time to define your learning outcomes and link them to the competency unit. An outcome would follow the words 'on completion of the project I will be able to ...'. Each outcome needs a verb, such as '*apply* a model for conflict management to ...' or 'analyse the responses of the candidates to the ...'.

Identify how you will approach the research or action learning project

At this stage you need to analyse what needs to be done. This includes library research, interviews with key people, reviews of documentation, assimilation of available statistics etc.

This is a most useful time to do a detailed task analysis of all the things that need to be done and the critical dates by which they need to be completed.

A Gantt chart is most useful for this purpose. This will soon let you know whether you are taking on too much for the time available. Don't forget about response times for surveys, word processing etc.

Finalize the outcomes of the work

In the example provided, one of the outcomes was a training manual with associated training resources. The report and presentation are compulsory parts of the assessment. When accompanied by materials such as those in the example, the report would not have to be as extensive as that produced by research. Other outcomes could be procedures manuals, plans, spreadsheets, minutes of meetings, videotapes or work related documents.

Negotiate the criteria for assessment with your trainer

The assessment criteria are used to decide whether your assignment/evidence has achieved the unit purpose. You must demonstrate in your report that you are able to integrate theory and practice, present and analyse the findings of your research or action project, and possibly develop recommendations. The use of report writing style, including numbered headings and logical format, index, referencing in the text and bibliography should all be familiar. In summary, the assessment criteria must cover the *presentation* and the *content* of your work. The criteria are a guide to you and the assessor to decide whether you have met the unit purpose.

Some examples of assessment criteria are listed:

- Headings and subheadings are used for logical presentation

- Theoretical principles are integrated, with referencing in the text

- Graphics and tables are used to illustrate data

- Data are analysed logically and consistently

- Job descriptions demonstrate an understanding and application of job satisfaction principles

- Procedures are consistent with quality management principles

- Training resources are clearly presented for overheads and handouts

- Recommendations are realistic and achievable

- Spreadsheets link common data

- Recommendations meet the requirements of relevant legislation.

Assessment criteria are the basis for self-assessment at the end of the project and for the feedback provided by your trainer.

Review and conclude negotiations for the learning contract

Before signing the learning contract review it briefly. You will be assessed against the criteria listed in the contract.

Start work on the research or activity

You will be surprised how the development of your learning contract has already led you along the pathway to completion of this work, as by now you will have a clear idea of where you are going and should not experience the writer's block most learners talk about with conventional assignments. Having planned tasks and deadlines to see that the project is achievable, you will have a number of urgent tasks to perform.

Plan activity or develop research instrument/report outline

The importance of planning your approach, and the form that your report will take, cannot be stressed enough. Take surveys for example. Very few learners realize how hard it is to analyse the results of a survey adequately. Many start off with a survey which asks everybody everything, leaving them with too much data to cope with. One learner decided to analyse service dimensions across a number of sectors in the hospitality industry. There were seven dimensions and four sectors. The permutations of this are enormous, as all the data need to be analysed.

If you look at the table below, the data in each of the cells would have to be analysed.

Service dimensions	Clubs	Restaurants	Hotels	Motels
Efficiency				
Friendliness				
Reliability				
Courtesy				
Value				
Guidance				
Attentiveness				

Comparisons between the sectors and graphs to illustrate each would be very extensive. This was not all this learner asked about in the survey, as data were collected on age, sex, country of origin and income. How would all this be integrated with the data in the table above to produce meaningful results? How would you ensure that conclusions reached were valid? If you only had two young male Japanese respondents, one in the restaurant sector and one in the hotel sector, what would this tell you about Japanese tourists? You can only draw conclusions when your sample is adequate. There are numerous books on research, and the chapter on sampling is most important.

Develop your report outline before you go ahead

It is amazing how the development of a report outline can focus your activity. In the case mentioned above, headings for the analysis of the data and a plan for how the data will be presented statistically and graphically will give you valuable direction. If you decide on your headings and follow the traditional format of introduction (aim, background and method), findings, discussion, conclusions you can't go very wrong. Learners on action learning projects may follow a more flexible format, but providing an introduction, background information, explanation of the activity, discussion of outcomes and conclusion is still one of the most logical approaches to take. Establishing your headings beforehand helps to ensure that you don't get sidetracked.

Index

For Product Safety Concerns and Information please contact our EU
representative GPSR@taylorandfrancis.com
Taylor & Francis Verlag GmbH, Kaufingerstraße 24, 80331 München, Germany

www.ingramcontent.com/pod-product-compliance
Ingram Content Group UK Ltd.
Pitfield, Milton Keynes, MK11 3LW, UK
UKHW051833180425
457613UK00022B/1234